YORK NOTES

The Merchant's Prologue & Tale

Geoffrey Chaucer

Notes by Pamela M. King

 Longman   York Press

The right of Pamela M. King to be identified as Author of this work has been asserted by her in accordance with the Copyright, Designs and Patents Act 1988

York Press
322 Old Brompton Road, London SW5 9JH

Pearson Education Limited
Edinburgh Gate, Harlow,
Essex CM20 2JE, United Kingdom
Associated companies, branches and representatives throughout the world

First published 2003

10 9 8 7 6 5 4 3 2 1

ISBN 0-582-77230-3

Designed by Vicki Pacey
Phototypeset by Land & Unwin (Data Sciences), Northampton
Produced by Pearson Education North Asia Limited, Hong Kong

CONTENTS

PART ONE

INTRODUCTION

HOW TO STUDY A NARRATIVE POEM

Studying a narrative poem on your own requires self-discipline and a carefully thought-out work plan in order to be effective.

- You will need to read the poem more than once. Start by reading it quickly for pleasure, then read it slowly and thoroughly.
- Look up all the words which you do not know. Some may have more than one meaning so note them. They may be intended to be ambiguous.
- On your second reading make detailed notes on the plot, characters and themes of the poem. Further readings will generate new ideas and help you to memorise the details.
- Think about how the poem is narrated. From whose point of view are the events described? Does your response to the narrator change at all in the course of the poem?
- The main character is the narrator, but what about the others? Do they develop? Do you only ever see them from the narrator's point of view?
- Identify what styles of language are used in the poem.
- Assess what the main arguments are in the poem. Who are the narrator's main opponents? Are their views ever fairly presented?
- Are words, images or incidents repeated so as to give the work a pattern? Do such patterns help you to understand the poem's themes?
- What is the effect of the poem's ending? Is the action completed and closed, or left incomplete and open?
- Does the poem present a world or point of view of which you are meant to approve?
- Cite exact sources for all quotations, whether from the text itself or from critical commentaries. Wherever possible find your own examples from the poem to back up your opinions.
- Always express your ideas in your own words.

These York Notes offer an introduction to *The Merchant's Prologue and Tale* and cannot substitute for close reading of the text and the study of secondary sources.

Fashionably dressed, self-controlled, with extensive business interests in England and abroad, Chaucer's Merchant is one of the *nouveau riches* of his era, if the description in the *General Prologue* is anything to go by. But apart from his financial worries, this pilgrim abruptly reveals a detail of his private life which leads on to his tale: two months before coming on the pilgrimage he made a disastrous mistake and married a woman who is making his life hell on earth.

His outburst is prompted within the drama of *The Canterbury Tales* by the Clerk's tale of Griselda, the meek woman who became the by-word for patience as she withstood the increasingly terrible trials to which her husband subjected her. In vain does the young, threadbare, shy and, presumably, celibate, scholar from Oxford protest that his tale is really an **allegory** of how human beings should submit to God's will; others, including Chaucer himself, insist on responding to its literal meaning. Their response relates back to the Wife of Bath, the wife from hell, to whom both Clerk and Merchant refer, whose colourful confession about how she has manipulated five successive husbands is fresh in the mind of pilgrim and reader alike.

Always one to turn outbursts to constructive advantage, Harry Bailey, the pilgrimage's genial host, suggests that the Merchant used his unfortunate experience of marriage as an opportunity to excel in the tale-telling competition. The reader never finds out what has gone wrong in the Merchant's marriage, but his tale tells of a classic mismatch between a wealthy – and lecherous – old man and a young gold-digger called May. As early as the wedding reception, the inevitable young lover, called Damian, appears on the scene. There is a description of just how unappealing the old husband, January, is in bed, and of the exchange of love letters and secret messages as the plot progresses to the expected conclusion. Other features are rather less predictable, such as the fact that January is struck inexplicably blind, then has his sight restored by the king of fairyland in time to catch May having sex with Damian up a pear tree.

The whole story is coloured by sustained **irony**, suggesting that the disillusioned Merchant cannot keep his own views out of the picture. In the final sexually explicit scene, he even apologises twice for causing offence, which simply attracts attention to the scene he is describing. What is obviously a comic tale at one level shows signs of aspiring to a serious message delivered by an embittered narrator, with the consequence that it verges on the distasteful. It narrowly avoids being pornographic, if not in the language it uses, then in the images it conjures up.

Just how much is the Merchant himself present in his tale, or does it actually reflect a middle-aged Chaucer's own views on marriage? Why is there such a long preliminary debate about the pros and cons of getting married at all? Does the reader care what happens to any of the characters, or are they all stupid, wicked or both? How far are they individuals? What other associations do January and May conjure up? Months of the year? Joseph and Mary? Adam and Eve? What is the significance of January's secret garden and, in particular, the pear tree, as a scene for adultery? And what on earth are the king and queen of the fairies doing in the plot at all? In the end, does *The Merchant's Tale* leave the reader in helpless fits of laughter or with a distinct sense of revulsion? Does it make a difference whether that reader is a man or a woman?

PART TWO

COMMENTARIES

The Merchant's Prologue and Tale is usually printed as the tenth of Chaucer's *Canterbury Tales*, the long sequence of framed stories on which he was working when he died. No version survives in Chaucer's own handwriting. Printing had not been invented when Chaucer was writing, so the earliest versions of *The Canterbury Tales* are all in manuscripts written by scribes for purchasers with different requirements. No two manuscripts are identical. It is not altogether clear which order Chaucer intended for the *Tales*, but conventionally the tales of the Clerk and the Merchant, which together form a linked fragment (Fragment IV), follow the fragment containing *The Wife of Bath's Prologue and Tale* to which they both refer.

The standard edition of the complete works of Chaucer is *The Riverside Chaucer*, edited by Larry D. Benson, Oxford University Press, 1988. These Notes are based on the single edition of *The Merchant's Prologue and Tale*, edited by Sheila Innes, Cambridge University Press, 2001.

SYNOPSIS

The Merchant introduced in the *General Prologue* seems a well-to-do figure. He sits high on his horse and is well dressed. He speaks authoritatively, and is a shrewd businessman, so no one guesses that he is in debt. It later emerges, when it is his turn to tell a tale, that he is recently and unhappily married.

The tale is set in Lombardy, where January, an elderly merchant, decides to take a wife. He thinks that marriage to a young woman will give him unlimited sex, protect his immortal soul, and secure him an heir. The Merchant narrator intervenes to ridicule this naivety.

January tells his two friends, Placebo and Justinus, of his plans. Placebo agrees with him, whereas Justinus warns him off. January continues to fantasise and eventually settles on marrying May, a young woman from the town.

The marriage is followed by a magnificent feast during which May attracts the attentions of Damian, January's young servant. The bride and groom retire to bed, where January makes love to May all night long. The narrator has no idea what May thinks of his efforts, as January is seriously unattractive.

Meanwhile Damian takes to his bed with love-sickness, after writing a love-letter to May which he keeps. When the newly-weds reappear in public, January discovers that his favourite servant is ill and sends May to visit him. Damian passes her his love-letter. May returns to her husband, then goes to the privy, where she reads and disposes of the letter. She resolves to take Damian as her lover and replies to that effect. He recovers and returns to work.

January makes a private garden for himself and May. The garden gate has only one key. Suddenly one day January is struck blind. Although he now never lets May out of reach, she borrows the garden key and makes an imprint of it in wax so that Damian can make a replica.

Then one day, when January and May go into the garden, Damian slips in ahead of them and hides. Unbeknown to everyone else, the king and queen of fairyland are watching what is going on. The king resolves to restore January's eyesight by magic, while the queen vows to equip May with such powers of argument that she will persuade January into disbelieving what he sees.

May develops a craving for pears and persuades January to let her climb on his back to reach them. Damian awaits her in the tree, immediately pulls up her clothes and they make love. The king of the fairies now restores January's sight and, looking upwards, he sees what is going on and shrieks in horror. May tells him that she was advised that struggling with a man in a tree would restore her husband's eyesight, and that January is just disorientated. January apologises, May leaps down from the tree, they kiss and make up and the tale ends.

Shocked, the Host reflects on his own marriage. He would love to tell the assembled company about his wife's many failings except she would be bound to find out, so he lets the matter go and the tale-telling competition moves on.

GENERAL PROLOGUE

LINES 272–86 Describing a well-to-do but inscrutable pilgrim

Sitting on a high horse was a Merchant with a forked beard, dressed in multi-coloured clothes, a fur hat, and boots with decorative clasps. He talked authoritatively about business and the need to keep shipping-lanes open. He was engaged in currency trading and was in debt, though his appearance did not betray it. He seemed respectable, but the narrator did not know his name.

The period when Chaucer was writing *The Canterbury Tales* was one which saw a steady growth in the number and status of people whose wealth came from trade, yet the medieval understanding of social rank was still formally one that equated wealth and status with land ownership. Land was easier to see, and therefore to tax, than moveable goods and cash. This Merchant seems well-to-do and authoritative, but ultimately he is impossible to place. He is part of what was an increasingly fluid social hierarchy. The major trade in the period was with the Low Countries – modern Belgium and the Netherlands – which is why the Merchant is concerned about protecting sea-routes between Middleberg, now in the south of the Netherlands, and Orwell, a trading port on the east coast of England. It also explains the origins of the hat, which completes his highly fashionable appearance. Merchants might often have all their wealth tied up in cargoes at sea, which were at risk not only from weather but from pirates and war. A merchant waiting for the profit on an export, or for the arrival of imported goods, might well have gone into debt. This Merchant is also involved in another kind of business, currency trading for profit, strictly illegal as a form of usury forbidden by the Bible, but commonly practised.

The portrait is, in the end, ambivalent. On the one hand, the reader is presented with an authoritative and fashionably dressed man. Yet he is not a member of the leisured classes, as he shows a preoccupation with matters relating to his work. He also has a much more fluid relationship with wealth, debt and sharp dealing practices than his appearance or conversation suggest.

berd beard
mottelee multi-coloured cloth
hye high
heed head
Flaundrissh Flemish (i.e. from modern-day Belgium)
bever beaver-skin
clasped fastened
fetisly elegantly
resons arguments
Sowninge consonant with
th'encrees the increase
winning profit
kept guarded
sheeldes *escus* (a French coin, with a shield on the obverse)
bisette employed, applied
wiste knew
wight person
estatly dignified
governaunce self-control
chevissaunce dealing, money-lending
For soothe in truth, indeed
sooth to seyn truth to tell
noot do not know

THE PROLOGUE OF THE MERCHANT'S TALE

LINES 1—32   **The Merchant is encouraged to turn his personal experience of the misery of marriage to advantage by telling a story on the subject**

The Merchant tells the Host that he has a terribly overbearing wife who would be more than a match for the devil himself if she were married to him. We are to be spared the detail, but suffice to say that she is very different from the paragon of meek patience which the Clerk has just described in his tale. This Merchant certainly won't marry again if he ever escapes his present trap. The single man whose body is ripped open is better off than the married man. And he has been married only two months. The Host replies that since the Merchant seems to know so much about unhappy marriage he should tell a tale on the subject. The Merchant agrees but refuses to say more of his own plight.

The Merchant's outburst is provoked by the Clerk's preceding tale in which Griselda, a paragon of patience, withstands all the excessive trials to which her husband subjects her. The unmarried Clerk has attempted to present his tale as an **allegory** of how humankind should accept the will of God, but others choose to take it literally. Chaucer's voice intervenes, telling women to stand up for themselves so as not to suffer like Griselda. The Host wistfully wishes his wife was like Griselda, then the Merchant responds by revealing that his wife of only two months is the very opposite of Griselda.

The failings he attributes to her are typical of the anti-feminist literature of the day (see Literary Background, Anti-Feminism). She is a 'shrewe' (line 10), a **metaphor** based on the observation that when they are trapped shrews screech and bite, and she is 'cursed' (line 27), carrying the sense both of hateful and evil. Her cursedness links her with the Devil, as her husband speculates on what a match she would make with Satan. In so doing he sets her up as the potential **antithesis** of Griselda in the allegorical sense, too, as good people in heaven are presented in the Bible, Revelations 21:9, as the brides of Christ. The vows a nun takes on permanently entering a convent are vows of a marriage to Christ. There are stories among the popular romances of Chaucer's day of women to whom terrible things happen when they have unwittingly been seduced by the Devil in disguise, but, the Merchant asserts, the Devil would be the sorry one were he to marry this woman. He swears by St Thomas of India, the disciple who had to touch the wounds of the resurrected Christ before he would believe in the Resurrection, implying that the Merchant himself had to try marriage before he would believe how bad it could be. It is worse than extreme physical violation. The voice of the Host intervenes to deflect the Merchant on to his tale on the subject, but there is nothing to suggest that the situation in the tale parallels the narrator's, beyond unsatisfactory marriage.

2 **on even and a-morwe** night and day
3 **Quod** said

Y

    mo more

4 **trowe** trust, believe

5 **woot** know

    fareth goes

7 **feend** fiend, the Devil

    ycoupled joined

8 **overmacche** outmatch

14 **unbounden** cut loose

    also moot I thee as I may thrive

15 **eft** afterwards

21 **ywedded be** been married

24 **rive** tear (apart)

32 **namoore** no more

THE MERCHANT'S TALE

LINES 33—54   Introducing January and his marriage ambitions

Once a rich sixty-year-old bachelor living in Lombardy became obsessed with getting married, even though he had previously enjoyed casual sex with whichever women he fancied. He declared, in his wisdom, that marriage, such as God devised for Adam and Eve in Paradise, was the only way to live.

> The tone of sustained **irony** is set from the beginning, as the narrator describes January as 'so wis' (line 54) when, given what he has told the pilgrims of his own predicament, this must be the reverse of what he thinks of anyone so eager to marry in their old age. January's change of heart is said to be the product of either religious scruple or senility, but the ironic tone points to the latter. Any contact with women, however casual, is described as the behaviour of secular fools, implying that the only real wisdom lies with monks and priests who take vows of chastity. The ironic relationship between the narrator and **protagonist** makes the reader's assessment of January a complex matter, but when we have access to him through direct speech we may suspect his motives; perhaps Chaucer is suggesting that the religious argument is a convenience for a randy old man who cannot pull women as easily as he used to. The reference to the Genesis story of the first marriage of Adam and Eve in Paradise is, however, **proleptic** of January and

May's later experience in their garden, just as the establishment that January is self-deluding here anticipates his later physical blindness.

33 **Whilom** formerly, once upon a time
   Lumbardye Lombardy (a region of modern Italy)
34 **Pavie** Pavia (also in Italy)
36 **wyflees** single, wifeless
37 **bodily delit** physical pleasure
38 **ther as was his appetit** wherever he desired
39 **seculeer** secular, not in religious orders
41 **Were it** whether it was
   hoolinesse piety
   dotage foolishness, senility
42 **swich** such
   corage desire, inclination
44 **dooth** does
   kan is able to
45 **T'espien where** to discover an opportunity through which
47 **thilke** this same
48 **bitwixe** between
49 **hooly boond** holy obligation
50 **bond** bound together
52 **esy** peaceable, suitable
   clene pure
54 **wis** wise

LINES $55-98$ The married and single life are compared

It is an excellent thing for an old man to take a young wife, particularly so that he can get an heir and live happily, unlike these young lads who mope about suffering from unrequited love. Young men think their liberty will bring them happiness in love, whereas the reverse is true. The married man, on the other hand, though bound by his marriage vows, enjoys the attentions of a wife, who is the most attentive and faithful kind of creature imaginable, who will in no circumstances leave him until his death. Some scholars, notably Theophrastus, disagree with this assessment, however, warning that a wife is only after a man's money.

Scholars debate whether these, and the hundred lines which follow, are spoken by January or by the Merchant. In Chaucer's time, the conventions of punctuation were less fixed than they have since become. As the tale survives in many copies, none of them in the author's handwriting, modern editors, and we as readers, have to make up our own minds. Generally the lines are given to the voice of the Merchant narrator, making this one of the longest passages of sustained **irony** in English literature.

In this section the physical contrast between the old, grey husband and the young, fair wife is established. The lot of the married man is juxtaposed with the conventional literary figure of the **courtly lover**, young, single and pining away because the object of his desire ignores him. The wife is described as the paragon of fidelity and attentive subservience suggested by the traditional Christian marriage vows. The underlying but persistent **imagery**, contrasting the liberty of the single life with the bondage of marriage, anticipates the later suggestion that 'until death us do part' can be a life-sentence. Note particularly the wordplay in the rhyming of 'ybounde' (line 73) (bound or constrained) and 'habounde' (line 74) (abound, overflow). *The Merchant's Tale* is unsurprisingly full of imagery based on trade, as well, as here where there is an ambiguous allusion to the wife as 'fruit' of his 'tresor' (line 58) meaning either that she is a man's most treasured possession, or his best buy.

The words of Theophrastus, the ancient commentator on marriage whose work is now lost, are dismissed as a lie, again an example of irony. He allegedly warned that a wife was motivated purely by greed, unlike a loyal servant or a good friend. Apart from robbery, the other risk is a wife's infidelity, which, given that she is the man's property, is the same thing, as it involves giving away what is rightly his to another man. Moreover, the attack on women is also ironic in a context where January is motivated by greed: for him a wife is a bargain because sex and service come free.

55 **sooth** truly
57 **namely** particularly
57 **hoor** hoary, grey-haired

59 **a feir** a beautiful (one)

60 **engendren** beget, conceive

61 **solas** comfort

63 **adversitee** setback, opposition

64 **nis** is not (contraction of 'not' and 'is' like modern 'isn't')

    childissh vanitee immature frivolity

65 **sit** is suitable, fitting

66 **peyne and wo** pain and unhappiness

67 **brotel** brittle, unstable

68 **wene** believe

    sikernesse security

69 **brid** bird

70 **arreest** constraint

71 **Ther as** whereas

    estaat condition, circumstances

72 **ordinaat** regulated, orderly

73 **yok** yoke (collar for harnessing working animals)

75 **buxom** submissive, obedient

76 **ententif** attentive, diligent

77 **sik and hool** ill and well, in sickness and in health

    make mate, partner

78 **For wele or wo** for good or ill, in good times and in bad

    wole will not want to

    forsake leave, abandon

79 **wery** tired

80 **bedrede** bedridden, confined to bed

    sterve dies

81 **clerkes** clerics, scholars

82 **Theofraste** Theophrastus

    oon of tho one of those

83 **What force** so what

    liste wants to

84 **housbondrye** household economy

85 **dispence** expenses

86 **dooth moore diligence** is more conscientious

87 **Thy good to kepe** to look after your possessions

90 **verray** genuine

knave servant

91 **bet** better

waiteth ay / After thy good is constantly waiting to inherit your possessions

94 **hoold** possession

95 **lightly** easily

mystow may you

cokewald cuckold, victim of adultery

96 **corse** curse

97 **take no kep** pay no attention to

98 **Deffie** defy

herke pay attention to

LINES 99—149   The true benefits and virtues of a wife

A wife is a gift from God, more permanent than a man's other possessions, which can come and go according to fortune. Marriage is a solemn sacrament of the Church, and I consider all unmarried men to be lost souls. After all, when God saw Adam naked and alone, he sent him Eve. This is proof that woman is intended to provide an earthly paradise for man. Husband and wife are as one flesh and one heart for better or worse, although how can any man have bad fortune if he has a wife? She does everything he tells her to and never disagrees. A man ought to get down on his knees and thank God for her, or, if he is unmarried, pray to be sent a wife. A man who takes his wife's advice cannot go wrong.

See Extended Commentaries, Text 1.

99 **yifte** gift

verraily truly, indeed

100 **hardily** assuredly

101 **londes** lands

commune rights over common land

102 **moebles** movable goods, furniture, household effects

103 **shadwe** shadow

106 **paraventure** perhaps

107 **ful greet sacrement** very important sacrament, ritual

108 **shent** ruined

111 **I sey nat this for noght** I mean this seriously

112 **ywroght** made

114 **bely-naked** stark naked

118 **preve** prove by experience

120 **paradis terrestre** earthly paradise

     disport comfort, entertainment

122 **moste nedes** must necessarily

123 **O** one

125 ***benedicite*** bless us!

126 **han** have

127 **Certes** certainly

128 **tweye** two

130 **povre** poor

     swinke work, labour

131 **kepeth** looks after

     never a deel not a bit

132 **lust** wants

     hire liketh weel pleases her well

135 **ordre** rank, class, state

136 **murye** merry

     eek also

138 **halt** holds, considers

144 **deceyved** deceived

145 **So that** so long as

     reed (rede) advice

146 **beren up his heed** hold up his head

147 **therwithal** in addition

148 **wolt werken as** want to behave like

LINES $150-81$ **Some examples and authorities to support the foregoing**

Look how Jacob got his father's blessing by doing as his mother advised, how Judith saved God's people by killing Holofernes, how Abigail saved her husband from death, how Esther arranged for her husband's promotion. Seneca says there is nothing better than a wife. Cato advises tolerating your wife's scolding because she will look after your household. The sick man without a wife is truly sorry. Love your wife as Christ loved the Church, as

y

you love your own self. Married couples have the right way of life: no harm can come to them, especially not to the wife.

In manuals of medieval preaching, once the theme of a sermon had been established, the preacher was advised to give examples drawn from the Old and New Testaments, from mythology and legend, and from everyday life. The narrator here, in offering evidence to support his premise, **parodies** that technique. The first three examples are drawn from the Bible and **Apocrypha**. The knowledgeable reader will be aware that Rebecca connived with her favoured son Jacob in deceiving her husband, when he was blind and on his deathbed, into depriving Esau, his firstborn and favourite son, of his rightful inheritance (Genesis, 27). Judith's legendary heroism arises because she saved her people by seducing Holofernes then decapitating him as he slept (Apocryphal Book of Judith, 14). Abigail successfully pleaded for the life of her husband Nabal, but her pleas charmed King David so much that he later married her when Nabal had died (1 Samuel, 25). Esther, like Judith, saved a people by betraying her man. In this case she persuaded the king to replace Mordechai who was condemned to die, with Haman who was hanged instead. The message is clear: either the narrator is a very poor biblical scholar, or the passage is heavily **ironic**, as all the paragons of female virtue share one characteristic and that is that each betrayed a man who had placed particular trust in her, albeit for some greater good.

The ironic thrust of the second verse-paragraph is less subtle. Here the narrator, allegedly quoting the ancient classical authorities Seneca and Cato, advises that if a man does everything his wife says, hands over all his goods to her management, and loves her as if they were one and the same person, no harm will befall him. The final line turns the passage around and makes the irony plain by modifying this assertion: no harm will befall the wife, at any rate.

150 **Lo** Look!
151 **conseil** counsel, advice
     his mooder Rebekke his mother Rebecca
153 **his fadres benison he wan** he won his father's blessing
156 **And slow him Olofernes** and killed Holofernes

161 **Mardochee** Mordechai
162 **Of Assuere enhaunced** promoted by Ahasuerus
163 **gree superlatif** greatest favour
164 **Senek** Seneca
165 **bit** bade, instructed
167 **of curteisye** out of good manners
169 **biwaille** bewail, lament
170 **Ther as ther nis no** where there is not any
171 **thou wolt wirche** you want to behave
175 **fostreth** nurture, care for
    thee thrive
176 **jape or pleye** joke or fool around
178 **siker** secure, certain, sure
179 **knit** joined together
180 **bitide** befall, happen
181 **upon the wyves side** of the wife's half

LINES $182-256$ January issues instructions for the finding of a wife for himself

January, having decided that marriage is desirable, sends for his friends to tell them what he intends. He tells them of his fear, as he nears death, that he has abused his body. Marriage will save his soul. He calls on their help to find him a young wife because he is in a hurry. She must be under twenty years old and pliable like wax to his needs. Old widows are to be avoided as they know many tricks to manipulate men. His wife must satisfy him sexually, otherwise he will be tempted into adultery. She must be able to bear him children so that his wealth does not fall into strange hands when he dies. He knows that in general, it is said, men should marry for procreation and for mutual assistance, not for lust. Sex should be viewed as a duty, but otherwise a couple should live chastely. January is not like that; he feels sexually vigorous, and the only sign of age is his grey hair. He is a fruit tree in full blossom.

> Chaucer here uses the device of January addressing his friends to give the reader further access to the character's voice. The **irony** in the reporting of January's speech is achieved by the opposition between

y

what he says about the religious motives for his marriage, and the imagery he employs when fantasising about his wife-to-be. He claims that he needs a young wife in order to satisfy himself sexually and to avoid adultery, which is forbidden in the Ten Commandments and is, therefore, a sure path to hell. He also wishes to conceive children to provide himself with heirs and because procreation, provided that sex is viewed as the necessary duty or 'debt' that each partner owes the other, is the pious purpose of marriage. The imagery, however, returns the reader to the market place, this time to the purchase of food (see Language and Style, on Imagery). The young wife is to be bought, owned and consumed as 'yong flessh' (line 206), 'tendre veel' (line 208). He, on the other hand, is the mature predatory pike. Older women, whom he dismisses as unacceptable, are presented as equivalent to the leftovers after the harvest, useful only as food and bedding for animals (see Themes, on Anti-Feminism). January's haste to marry is, therefore, delightfully ambivalent: is he really fearful of impending death and hell, or is he in a lather of sexual anticipation?

His justification is supported by **proverbial** wisdom, but he is apparently unaware of the proverb underpinning the narrator's earlier **encomium** on marriage: 'marry in haste, repent at leisure' (see Language and Style, on Speech). The imagery of this passage also functions **proleptically**, as Chaucer uses one of his favourite comic techniques by introducing an idea through an **image, simile** or **metaphor** early in a story, in anticipation of its actual appearance. Wax features in the tale later as May makes a mould of the key to the garden to give access to her secret young lover, and the consequent adultery takes place in a fruit tree. January's comparison of himself to a fruit tree, blooming, apparently miraculously, in old age, also refers outside the poem to the **apocryphal** legend of how old Joseph came to be betrothed to young Mary with a rather different outcome (see Themes, on Joseph and Mary/Adam and Eve). In dismissing pious generalisations about the purpose of marriage, January complains that those who wrote them know as little about marriage as does his page-boy, again ironically anticipating Damian's sexual success with May. Consequently key elements of the later deception of January are anticipated in the imagery of this passage.

182 **inwith his dayes olde** in his old age

183 **vertuous quiete** virtuous peacefulness

186 **hem** them

th'effect of his entente the essence of his intentions

187 **sad** serious, sober

189 **woot** knows

on my pittes brinke on the edge of my grave, i.e. near death

191 **folily despended** foolishly wasted

194 **anoon** immediately, straight away

in al the haste I kan as quickly as I am able to

196 **shapeth for** arrange for, provide for

197 **I wol nat abide** I do not want to wait

198 **I wol fonde t'espien** I will try to discover

200 **forasmuche as** insofar as

mo more (in number)

201 **Ye shullen rather** you are more able

202 **allyen** make an alliance

204 **in no manere** by any means, at all

205 **passe** be more than

206 **ful fain** very willingly

207 **pyk** pike

pikerel young pike

210 **bene-straw** dried beanstalks (i.e. inedible, animal bedding)

greet forage bulk winter food for animals

211 **widwes** widows

212 **konne so muchel craft** are expert in so many cunning devices

Wades boot Wade's boat (aspects of the reference are obscure, but it appears to refer to a boat with special properties of deception belonging to Wade, a legendary Germanic hero)

213 **broken harm** petty annoyances

215 **scoles** schools of thought, methodologies

sotile cunning, subtle

217 **gye** guide

218 **wex** wax

plye shape, mould

219 **in a clause** in brief

221 **if so were** if it happened

222 **ne koude** was unable to
plesaunce (sexual) pleasure
223 **avoutrye** adultery, sexual infidelity
226 **levere** rather
229 **I dote nat** I am not feeble-minded
woot know
232 **page** young manservant, page-boy
234 **he ne may nat** he is unable to
235 **devocioun** reverence, moral earnestness
236 **leveful procreacioun** allowable breeding, the production of legally acknowledged offspring
238 **paramour** love-making
239 **eschue** reject, avoid
240 **yelde hir dette** pay their debt (i.e. the marital obligation of sex)
242 **meschief** mischance, difficulty
245 **avaunt** boast
246 **lymes** bodily parts
stark strong, powerful
247 **bilongeth** belongs, appertains
249 **fare** get on, do, seem
250 **blosmeth** blossoms
er before
ywoxen grows
253 **grene** green
254 **laurer** laurel
thurgh through
sene be seen
255 **sin** since

LINES $257-306$ January just hears the advice he wants

Sundry men offer January conflicting advice on marriage, drawing on all manner of examples, but in the end the matter becomes a debate between his two friends, Placebo and Justinus. Placebo tells him that he showed the wisdom of Solomon in seeking advice, but that in the end January is wise enough himself to know what to do. Placebo has been at court all his life and, despite his unworthiness, has made progress in his career by never disagreeing with his social superiors. In his view, January has shown such great good sense that he supports him absolutely in his ambition to take a young wife.

> By this point in the narrative the reader has formed a view of January, and the major fields of **imagery** have been established. Major points of debate have also been introduced: whether marriage, especially in old age, is a risk or a benefit, and what is the true purpose of marriage. Support for the arguments on all sides have been drawn from popular proverbial wisdom and learned authority, undercut throughout by the construction of the Merchant, an obtrusive narrator allegedly drawing on direct personal experience. This passage opens by indicating that there is a lot of conflicting advice available which, in the end, offers nothing but confusion and uncertainty. In this passage the whole question of advice is brought to a close, as the narrative **mode** turns to **personification allegory**. January's two friends from whom he seeks advice have significant names, Placebo and Justinus, They represent not only the two sides of the debate on marriage, but two kinds of friendly advice: Placebo here offers flattery. He also expresses the view that wise men should not presume to advise their elders and social superiors if they want to get on in life. Placebo is the archetypal flatterer, familiar to Chaucer's original audience from court **satire** (see Characterisation on Characters in the tale). Note how his manner of speaking, full of **clichés** and meaningless tags, reflects the emptiness of his so-called advice.

262 **al day** always, all the time, generally

263 **disputisoun** discussion, debate

264 **cleped** called, named

Placebo (Latin, literally 'I shall please')

265 **Justinus** (derived from Latin, suggesting one who offers just advice)

269 **sapience** wisdom

270 **yow ne liketh** it doesn't please you

271 **weyven** waver, depart

277 **bringe at reste** bring to a peaceful destination

279 **motif** proposition, motive

283 **degree** rank

284 **estaat** social position

286 **contraried** contradicted

288 **semblable** similar

291 **dar** dare

292 **passe** surpass

293 **by my fay** by my faith, upon my soul

295 **sentence** sense

296 **everydeel** every bit

300 **halt** held

302 **stapen** advanced

303 **by my fader kin** upon my father's family

304 **hangeth on a joly pin** is cheerfully tuned

305 **matiere** business

leste like, choose, please

LINES $307-64$ **January receives a warning which he chooses to ignore**

Justinus hears Placebo out then asks if he can offer his advice. Citing Seneca, he reminds January that if he must be careful with his goods, he should be even more careful with his body. He should first look into the vices and virtues of any prospective wife, for, though no one is perfect, she should have more of the latter than the former. He counsels caution, for his own marriage has not been altogether happy, although neighbours, particularly women, tell him he has an excellent wife. For an old man to marry a young woman is risky, as even a young man would be hard pressed to satisfy his wife. He gives January's marriage three years. January, supported by Placebo, dismisses this advice, and decides finally to marry when and whom he pleases.

> Justinus appears to hold views based on personal experience which are similar to those of the Merchant narrator. Rather than seeing these as individual opinions, however, they should be recognised as a compilation drawn from contemporary anti-feminist literature (see Themes, on Anti-Feminism). In particular, the virtues and vices which the still non-existent candidate for January's hand in marriage

might have are drawn from this body of writing. For example, women are portrayed as hypocritical, so that the husband's grief is based on private conflict while everyone around believes that his wife is perfect. The vices women may show are all associated with incontinence of some kind: drunkenness, excessive shrill talking and scolding, and sexual voraciousness. The last is the biggest threat, based on a belief that once women had tasted the delights of sex they could never have enough of it, that they would wear out even a young man, and no one man will be enough for one woman for long.

Despite Justinus' assertion that his advice is born of personal experience, January dismisses it as so much book learning, which, at one remove, is precisely what it is. The outcome, that January prefers Placebo's 'advice', enacts the view that no matter how much accumulated wisdom there is available, human beings, particularly in matters concerning sex and marriage, have to make their own mistakes. Just as January dismisses 'scole-termes' (line 357), so, too, the approved manner by which scholars attempted to arrive at the truth is undercut. University philosophers in the Middle Ages favoured dialectic, the 'sic et non' (thus and not thus), whereby two sides of an argument were tested. The whole debate on marriage in *The Merchant's Tale* is no debate at all, however, as no one enters it with an open mind. The implication must be that decisions regarding the relationship between the sexes are governed by something other than logic.

313   **yeveth** gives

     lond land

     catel property

317   **alwey** always, ever

320   **enquere** investigate

321   **dronkelewe** habitually drunk

322   **shrewe** shrill and bad-tempered (as shrews are, reputedly)

323   **chidestere** scold, nag

324   **mannissh wood** man-mad

326   **trotteth hool in al** is perfect in everything

330   **thewes** personal qualities

331   **axeth leyser** demands leisure, time

336   **observances** duties, matters for attention

338 **route** crowd

341 **where wringeth me my sho** where my shoe pinches

342 **mowe** may

348 **Is bisy ynough** has his work cut out

353 **yvele apaid** dissatisfied

356 **panyer ful of herbes** basket of vegetables (i.e. I couldn't give a fig)

357 **scole-termes** technical scholarly arguments

361 **letteth matrimoigne** prevents marriage

LINES $365-404$ **Determined to marry, January chooses his own wife unaided**

January becomes greatly preoccupied with choosing his wife by day and fantasises by night about many of the young women who live nearby, holding up a mental mirror to the marketplace through which they pass. He weighs up their rival attractions of body and temperament as well as their reputations. Eventually he chooses one, without consulting anyone else, for love is blind. Considering all her attractions, he is pleased with his choice, and calls his friends together again to tell them he has no more need of their help in the matter.

> Chaucer uses the **proverb** 'love is blind' (line 385) to shape his portrait of January as the self-deluding old lecher, whose blindness to the kind of woman he has chosen anticipates his actual physical blinding. January, whose 'bisynesse' (line 365) again suggests an unhealthy obsession with sex, chooses his wife as if he were buying meat, considering the available local women as goods in the marketplace. The **image** of the mirror is commonplace in the literature of the time, where art is promoted as a mirror of reality in a number of ways. Here the mirror is in January's imagination, however, making him a mental voyeur, secretly ogling the local young women. The anti-feminist book on which Chaucer draws most extensively in the tale is a work by his French contemporary Eustace Deschamps entitled *Le Miroir de Mariage* ('The Mirror of Marriage') reflecting a very different picture of women from that which is depicted as passing through January's head at this juncture (see Themes, on Anti-Feminism). The list of attractions he finds in the available talent complements the list of vices projected by Justinus in the preceding passage. He considers beauty,

popularity and reputation, finally settling on one whose attributes are drawn from the classic picture of a desirable woman in **courtly romance**. She is young and beautiful, with a narrow waist, long slender arms, self-possession, refined manners, womanly deportment and suitable gravity. He is very pleased with himself, but the quality of his choice is immediately undercut when it is described as a fantasy by the narrator. January having heard only the advice he wanted to hear, now sees only what he wants to see.

365 **curious bisynesse** elaborate activity
366 **gan** did
  impresse make a mark
370 **As whoso** as if someone
374 **devise** reflect on
378 **stant** stood
  grace favour
379 **sadnesse** sobriety, seriousness
  beningnitee goodness, graciousness
380 **grettest voys** best reputation
381 **badde name** bad reputation
383 **apointed** decided, settled
384 **goon** go
385 **chees** chose
387 **ybroght** conveyed
388 **purtreyed** pictured, imagined
390 **middel** waist
391 **governaunce** behaviour
  gentillesse refined kindness
393 **beringe** deportment
393 **condescended** settled, agreed
402 **abregge** reduce, shorten

LINES 405–42 January defends his choice to his friends but voices certain anxieties

January calls his friends together and begs them not to contest his choice. He says he has chosen a girl from the town, whose physical attractions make up for her lack of social class. He looks forward to the fact that marriage will mean he has her all to himself. He then confides, however, that his conscience troubles him, because he understands that he will be so blissfully happy in marriage that God may decide he has had his heaven on earth, and send him to hell when he dies. He asks for his friends' reassurance on this point.

> This passage is **tonally** interesting for some of the superficially inconsequential details it includes, which carry a number of inferences about the quality of January's choice of wife. Despite the fact that all manner of courtly graces have just been attributed to the chosen lady, the reader and January's friends now learn that he has settled for someone of low social standing because of her surpassing physical attraction. The dangers inherent in this, from the point of view of the very hierarchical society of Chaucer's time, that she may be a gold-digger whose behaviour may not be very ladylike, is reinforced by the detail that she lives in the town, carrying the suggestion of **euphemism** akin to 'of the streets' in present day English. At any rate she is neither high-born, nor a country innocent. January also thanks God that marriage will mean he does not have to share her, carrying the implication that her sexual favours might otherwise be available for sharing.

> This section of the passage is in **free indirect speech** so that some of January's attitudes are conveyed through his actual words whilst simultaneously being undermined by the sceptical reporting of the controlling narrative voice. The following direct speech then helps to build up anticipation of what is to come through further techniques of **irony**. January's description of his anticipated marriage not only states that it will be blissful, but provides the alternative possibility 'wo and stryf' (line 434), albeit in the negative. As these words trigger the reader's recollection of the Merchant's description of his marriage, January on cue asserts that 'alle wedded men' (line 439) live in happiness with their wives, fatally undermining his credibility. Moreover, the idea that marriage will be heaven on earth, and that January's immortal soul will thereby be threatened by such excessive happiness is ludicrous. The attentive reader of the whole of *The Canterbury Tales* will also remember that the Wife of Bath (lines

489–90) speculates that she gave her late husbands such a bad time in this life that she probably secured them a place in heaven when they died. The spurious debate on the relationship between earthly and heavenly bliss depends on understanding a theology in which a place in heaven has to be earned through purgatorial experiences either in this life, or after death in a part of the afterlife designated for the purpose.

406 **alderfirst** first of all

    boone favour

410 **verray ground** true foundation

417 **he mighte han hire al** he might have her totally to himself

425 **ful yoore ago** a very long time ago

426 **parfite blisses two** two perfect happinesses (i.e. on earth and in heaven)

428 **the sinnes sevene** the Seven Deadly Sins (i.e. those guaranteed to bring human beings to hell: pride, covetousness, anger, envy, lechery, gluttony and sloth)

429 **thilke tree** that same tree (in penitential literature, the sins and virtues were conventionally represented diagrammatically as trees)

434 **delicat** luxurious, refined

437 **penaunce** a sacrament of the Church whereby sins are atoned for through the performance of unpleasant tasks

440 **Assoileth** solve, resolve

LINES 443–76   Justinus reassures January that his immortal soul is unlikely to be at risk

Justinus comes straight to the point and tells January that it is extremely unlikely that marriage will prevent him from achieving heaven. Indeed, a wife could be God's mysterious way of ensuring that a man has sufficient purgatory on earth that he may go straight to heaven. He warns January not to indulge himself excessively in sex and to avoid other sins, and reminds him that the Wife of Bath has already told the company succinctly what marriage is really like.

> The narrative construct which separates the characters within the tales from the characters on the Canterbury pilgrimage (see Characterisation) appears to break down here, as Justinus, a character within the tale, and, therefore, located somewhere in Lombardy in the indeterminate past, refers to the Wife of Bath, one of the

Canterbury pilgrims, as being 'on honde' (line 473). The fact that this does not unduly matter, rather than suggesting that Chaucer has made a mistake or lost control of his elaborate creation, demonstrates that *The Canterbury Tales* is not a fully-realised drama. Justinus, an **allegorical figure** representing plain truth-telling, shares views and experience of marriage, as well as a certain abruptness of manner, which coincide with those of the Merchant narrator. There are a number of ways of describing what is going on here as a result. Justinus can be described as the Merchant's surrogate in the tale, or it might be said that the narrative boundary between the frame and tale is permeable, or that the narrative is secondary to argument at this point in the book.

The message mockingly delivered to January is that God is known to work in mysterious ways and may yet turn out to have set up this marriage as a trial and an opportunity for January to win a place in heaven. January would know this if he had been paying attention to the Wife of Bath. The sophisticated literary joke is that January is now being criticised not only for living in his own private fantasy world, but for being a character locked within *The Merchant's Tale*, so lacking the accumulated worldly wisdom of the Canterbury pilgrims, themselves also fictional characters.

Justinus' refusal to refer to learned authorities to support his argument, in order to save time, dramatises a certain exasperation with the futility of trying to convince a deluded character like January by any means, and also signals to the audience that the debate on marriage is drawing to a close. The desire to finish the tale and 'waden out' (line 472) of the business may be read as coincidentally shared by Justinus, by the Merchant, and by Chaucer recognising the need to get on with the story.

444 **japerye** joking
446 **auctoritee** authority (i.e. as written by ancient authors)
   allegge adduce
450 **youre right of hooly chirche** your rite in the holy church (i.e. your funeral)
451 **repente of** regret
455 **Wel ofte rather** much more often
458 **purgatorie** Purgatory (i.e. the physical location in the other world often

depicted as a mountain which souls have to climb while being put through a
number of painful trials in order to reach heaven)

459   **meene** intermediary, medium, go-between

465   **lette of** be deprived of

467   **attemprely** temperately, with moderation

470   **tak** (some editions read **tale**) account, contribution to the debate

472   **Beth nat agast** don't worry

473   **waden out** move on from

LINES 477–529 January and May get married

January's friends take their leave in order to arrange his wedding to the girl,
whose name is May. The narrator will not go into the legal details of the
marriage settlement or the fine clothes for the occasion; suffice to say that
they were duly married by a priest in the customary way. The wedding feast
was superlative in every way, surpassing those of myth and legend. The
gods were delighted. The narrator challenges Marcianus Capella, the
Roman poet, to find words to describe this marriage of age with youth.

At last the reader meets the bride. Her name is May, suggesting more
allegorical characterisation, as it is now clear that 'winter' is marrying
'late spring' (see Themes, on Calendars and Astrology). The contrast is
later summed up: 'tendre youth hath wedded stouping age' (line 526).

The **lexical fields** in this passage are interesting: legal vocabulary
reminds us that this marriage is a transaction, a binding commercial
contract by which May is given a permanent interest in January's
lands. These details are swiftly followed by an almost desultory
description of the marriage itself, where the vocabulary associated
with the solemn sacrament contrasts with the bald **paratactic syntax**
of the single sentence devoted to the ceremony. There then follows
an extravagant description of the wedding feast, drawing exaggerated
analogies with pagan classical examples. We are told that Venus,
goddess of sexual love, is present, dancing in front of the couple. In
Chaucer's time pagan gods were frequently incorporated into
narratives with an otherwise Christian perspective. Conflict is avoided
because the pagan deity comes to stand as an allegory for a particular
property or attribute, and, as is the case with Venus, also operates as a

personification of a planet understood to exert some particular astrological influence. An account liberally embellished with classical allusions, such as this passage would not be out of place in the **high style rhetoric** of **romances,** as is the case in *The Knight's Tale*, but here it is flanked by low style passages of realism which expose it as being as pretentious as January's fantasies.

Taking the passage as a whole, the true solemnity of the marriage ceremony is cursorily sandwiched between an account of the legal settlement, clearly the bride's overriding interest, and the luxurious feast which stands in as a kind of sensual foreplay for January as he looks forward to enjoying his bride. Again mercantile **imagery** and food imagery, both types of consumption, characterise this rather unholy transaction. The narrator has the last word when he concludes that no poet can do justice to such 'mirthe' (line 527), a deeply **ambiguous** word suggesting that the marriage may be delightful or laughable.

480   **by sly and wys tretee** by cunningly devised and shrewd agreement
481   **which that Mayus highte** who was called May
484   **trowe** believe
485   **to longe yow to tarie** too long to hold you up for
486   **scrit** written document
       bond formal pledge, obligation
487   **feffed in** enfeoffed, put in possession of
488   **herknen of** listen to an account of, pay attention to
       array clothes
491   **stole** stole (ecclesiastical garment put on by the priest performing the sacrament and wound round the couple's hands in the ceremony when they are 'handfasted' or bound together in God's eyes)
492   **Sarra and Rebekke** Sarah and Rebecca (Biblical examples of faithful wives)
493   **trouthe** fidelity
494   **orisons** prayers
       usage customary
495   **croucheth hem** made the sign of the cross over them
499   **deys** dais, platform on which the high table is placed
501   **instrumentz** instrumental music

vitaille provisions, food

502 **deyntevous** delicious, choice

504 **Orpheus** Orpheus (legendary harpist, half god)

Thebes Amphioun Amphion, King of Thebes (whose music helped build the city)

504 **minstralcye** music, accompanied singing

506 **tromped** trumpet

507 **Joab** Joab (legendary trumpeter in the Old Testament, II Samuel 2:28)

508 **Theodomas** Theodamas (Theban augur, whose predictions were accompanied by trumpeting)

510 **Bacus** Bacchus (Roman god of wine)

shinketh pours out

512 **hir knight** a knight owing special allegiance to her

513 **assayen his corage** test his spirit

518 **Ymeneus** Hymen (Roman god of maidenhood and marriage)

520 **Marcian** Marcianus Capella (Roman poet who wrote *De Nuptiis Philologiae et Mercurii*)

522 **Philologie** Philology (language)

Mercury Mercury (messenger of the gods)

523 **the Muses** the Muses (female deities who inspire the different arts by singing)

526 **stouping** stooping, bent, drooping

527 **mirthe** merriment, laughter

528 **witen** understand

LINES 530–82   Another man falls prey to May's charms

May is very beautiful and January cannot wait to get her into bed, although she worries whether she will be able to sustain his sexual energy. He contrives things so that the wedding guests finally prepare to leave. Everyone is very happy except January's household servant Damian, who is so smitten by the sight of May that he is nearly mad with desire. He is condemned to suffer until May takes pity on him. The narrator pauses to exclaim on the particular dangers of the enemy within.

The **hyperbole** and inflated **rhetoric** which characterises the narrator's description of the wedding feast now rises to a comic climax as Damian, January's household servant, falls madly in love with May. Accordingly, the scene is set for the adultery before the marriage is consummated, while the new husband is still fantasising about having his new wife in his arms in bed and worrying about whether she will be able to withstand his virility. The comparisons with legendary lovers become increasingly laughable in their inappropriateness: January is no Paris of Troy and May is compared with Esther, the Old Testament model of meek wifely beauty, yet the reader is presently told that Damian must suffer the pains of unrequited love *until*, not unless, she takes pity on him. Similarly Chaucer draws on the refined language of **courtly love** to describe Damian's sudden attraction to May, elevating the infatuation of a young servant for a girl plucked off the streets to the level of the knights and ladies of high **romance**. The incongruity which is the source of humour is not merely a product of social snobbery but of the mixing of literary **modes**, mingling the non-realistic exaggerated sentiments of romance, and the intervention of the gods in corporeal form, with homely details associated with normal medieval town life.

The rhetorical device of lines 571 onwards, **apostrophe**, is recommended by manuals of style, with which Chaucer is known to have been familiar, as suitable only for such contexts as funeral orations for the monarch. Throughout the tale, underlying biblical references suggest comparisons between January and May by turns with Joseph and Mary or with Adam and Eve. Whether May is going to play Mary to January's old Joseph or Eve to his Adam begins to resolve itself here as Damian is compared to an adder, the guise taken by the devil in the Garden of Eden when Eve was tempted into eating the forbidden fruit in the **archetypal** act of wifely betrayal (see Themes, on Joseph and Mary/Adam and Eve).

531 **faierye** magic, enchantment
532 **Ester** Esther (biblical queen noted for meekness – see Old Testament Book of Esther)
534 **Assuer** Ahasuerus (Old Testament king who took Esther as his second wife on account of her meek beauty)
538 **ravisshed in a traunce** infatuated by
540 **manace** threaten, menace
542 **Paris dide Eleyne** Paris did to Helen (the legendary rape of the Greek queen Helen by the Trojan prince Paris led to the Trojan War)

548 **susteene** withstand

550 **it were woxen night** night had fallen, it had grown dark

552 **ago** gone

555 **mete** food

555 **subtil wise** discreet ways

556 **resoun was to rise** it was reasonable to rise from table

561 **carf biforn** carved in front of (i.e. served his master with meat at high table)

563 **ny wood** nearly mad

564 **swelte** was overcome

565 **brond** firebrand

568 **Namoore** no more

569 **pleyne** lament

570 **rewen on** take pity on, regret

571 **bedstraw** (straw was used to stuff mattresses)
       bredeth arises, grows, breeds

572 **bedeth** waits

573 **false hoomly hewe** false domestic servant

574 **naddre** adder

578 **borne man** servant by birth (Damian was born into a family of estate servants)

580 **hoomly fo** familiar, intimate enemy, (lit.) enemy in the home

581 **pestilence** plague

LINES 583–653 January has May in his bed at last

The sun sets, night falls, and the wedding guests go home to their own private affairs. January drinks various potions to enhance his sexual prowess. The marriage bed is blessed, and the bride and groom are at length left alone together. January apologises to May for what he is about to do, but reassures her that there is no hurry, that they have all night, because sex is approved of within marriage. He then makes love to her until dawn, has a quick snack, sits up in his nightshirt and nightcap and sings loudly with delight. Who knows what May thinks, but she is not impressed. January then sleeps half the day, and May confines herself to her own room for four days, as is customary for newly married women.

See Extended Commentaries, Text 2.

583 **Parfourned** performed
       ark diurne daily arc

584 **sojourne** stay, delay

586 **On th'orisonte** on the horizon

587 **mantel** cloak

rude rough

588 **hemisperie** hemisphere

589 **lusty route** cheerful crowd

593 **hastif** impatient

595 **ypocras** hypocras (medicinal cordial named after Hippocrates, the Greek acknowledged as founding medical science)

clarree clary (a sweet, spiced wine)

vernage vernaccia (strong sweet Italian wine)

596 **t'encressen his corage** to increase his (sexual) desire, potency

597 **letuarie** remedy

598 **daun Constantin** Constantinius Afer of Carthage (the monk who brought Arab scientific learning to Salerno in Italy in the eleventh century)

599 ***De Coitu** On Sex* (Latin sex manual)

600 **he nas no thing eschu** he rejected nothing

601 **privee** personal, intimate

603 **voiden** empty, clear out

605 **travers** curtain, screen (creating private sleeping-quarters)

613 **houndfissh** dogfish

brere briar

616 **trespace** offend, injure

623 **no fors** it does not matter

630 **laboureth** toiled, exerted himself

631 **a sop of fyn clarree** bread soaked in sweet wine

634 **made wantown cheere** behaved amorously

635 **coltish** like a colt, friskily

ragerye lust, lechery

636 **jargon** chatter

637 **flekked pye** spotted magpie (noted for being noisy)

638 **chaunteth** chants

craketh croaks

639 **in her herte** inwardly

643 **pleying** love-play

645 **prime** the first hour (according to a way of measuring time based round the regular times for prayer in monasteries, usually around 9.00 a.m.)

649 **As usage is** as is customary

LINES 654–719 **January arranges for May to visit Damian on his sickbed**

The narrator turns his attention to Damian, speculating on his predicament. Damian writes May a verse-letter and keeps it next to his heart. When January and May finally reappear in public to dine, January notices Damian's absence from table and discovers that he is ill in bed. January is sorry, as he values Damian as a good servant, and kindly resolves that he and May should both visit him. He asks May to go first while he has a rest.

> The transition into this passage places the voice of the narrator in the foreground, as Chaucer builds comic suspense as the Merchant mockingly asks Damian what he is going to do next. The reader is by now prepared for the inevitable liaison between May and Damian, so the narrative interest lies in the mechanics of how it is to be effected. Damian's first move is to write a letter to May in verse, then not to send it but to place it in a silk purse next to his heart. Again the conventions of **courtly love** are being mocked, as in context the action seems both rather unnecessary and completely ineffectual, if comically affecting. Meanwhile the progress of January and May's relationship is embellished by reference to astrological changes in the heavens, as the reader is told that the moon, the planet of inconstancy, has moved into Cancer, the star-sign governing the month of May.

> The coming shift in the balance of power between January and May is anticipated by her description of being as fresh as a summer's day. Increasingly their incompatibility will be conveyed through the **imagery** of winter versus summer. Already in this passage we can see that one is active while the other is passive, which prepares the way for May to visit Damian unaccompanied by her husband. The passage is full of courtly vocabulary used to **ironic** effect: January's concern about Damian is attributed to the servant's fine qualities and manners, while January's solicitous decision that he should be visited on his sickbed by the lord and lady he serves is commended as a noble and generous gesture. The comically **proleptic** result is that May is instructed by her husband to go and entertain Damian in bed.

657 **sely** innocent

658 **Andswere to my demaunde** tell me this

661 **thy wo biwreye** reveal (the cause of) your sorrow

665 **in aventure** at risk

667 **penner** pen-case

669 **compleynt** song of lamentation (usually formal and stylised expression of unrequited love)

lay poem (usually rhymed and intended for singing)

675 **In two of Tawr** the second degree of Taurus

into Cancre into Cancer (via Gemini)

681 **heighe masse** high mass (the main religious service of the day, including the celebration of the eucharist)

688 **entendeth nat to me** is not waiting on me

689 **how may this bitide** how has this come about

693 **tarye** delay

694 **forthinketh** grieves, displeases

696 **routhe** a pity

699 **servisable** willing, useful

700 **thrifty** successful

705 **bountee** kindness, good deeds

708 **taak good hede** make sure, play attention that

709 **At after-mete** after dinner

712 **Dooth him disport** entertain him

714 **Have I no thing but rested me a lite** I have only to have a short rest first

718 **marchal** master of ceremonies

LINES 720–75   May discovers Damian's love and considers what to do next

May visits Damian and he secretly passes her his letter, begging her to keep his secret. May returns to January's bed, makes her excuses, goes and reads Damian's letter in the privy, tears it up and throws away the evidence. While she undresses so that January can make love to her, she contemplates what to do about Damian. Astrologically the time is ripe for love, so one way or another May decides to take pity on Damian and to love him above all others.

The narrator's voice dominates this passage. Twice he backs away from offering an opinion, Chaucer's technique for dramatising his disapproval. The same voice is, however, not squeamish about giving his audience the detail of May's visit to the privy, albeit by **circumlocution** and **euphemism**, or of January's requirement that she take off all her clothes.

The passage as a whole is a mixture of details which are laughably discordant. The poems of **courtly love** written by Damian are transported from the silk purse by his heart, via May's bosom, to the privy, a journey which may be read as emblematic of the course of both of May's relationships – both at the outset couched in sentiments connected with religion and refined feeling, but both ultimately being concerned with woman as a sexual commodity. A similar technique is the use of the device of **traductio**, whereby a single word, phrase or idea enters a text first of all in a metaphorical sense and later occurs in a much more prosaic and literal sense. Such is the case here with 'impression' (line 766): January wanted a young woman to be like wax so he could mould her to his will, now May has **ironically** had an impression made on her by Damian, but both **images** anticipate the actual impression in wax that May will make of the key to the secret garden in which her affair with Damian will be consummated.

May remains inscrutable. She sets off to see Damian promptly and later decides to be his lover however poor he may be, yet the narrator never reports that she has any feelings for either of the men in her life. In this misogynist narrative only men experience deeply-felt emotion; women are alien beings. This makes the statement that pity soon flows in the gentle heart problematic. It is generally read as ironic, as May is not gentle – that is 'high class' – by birth, and her motives could be the need to find a more satisfying sexual partner than January. The narrator is at pains to explore why events occur in the way they do, asserting that nothing happens without reason, while conveying the uneasy suspicion that some things, like sexual attraction, are simply inexplicable.

720 **yholde** taken
724 **say** saw
725 **bille** letter, petition
728 **siketh** sighs
730 **discovere** expose
731 **kid** made known

y

734 **ye gete namoore of me** that is all I am prepared to say

738 **she moste gon** she had to go

739 **Ther as ye woot that every wight moot neede** to the place you know everyone must need to go

741 **rente** tore

cloutes shreds

742 **privee** privy, latrine

softely quietly, tenderly

743 **studieth** ponders, takes thought

748 **dide hem encombraunce** were in his way

749 **be hire lief or looth** whether she liked it or not

750 **precious** fastidious

754 **Til evensong rong** until the bells rang for evensong

755 **by destinee or aventure** by fate or chance

756 **influence** power exercised by heavenly bodies

757 **constellacion** relative position of the planets, the stars

760 **alle thing hath time** everything has its time

763 **causelees** without cause, reason

764 **deme** judge

766 **impression** imprint

771 **rekke not** do not care

774 **renneth** flows

775 **franchise** generosity, liberality

LINES 776–808 May brings about Damian's recovery by agreeing to be his secret lover

The narrator suggests that like all decisions women take on their own, May's determination to love Damian is fortunate, as otherwise Damian might have died of love. May now writes a letter to Damian promising him all the sexual favours he desires if they can only find a suitable time and place. She puts it under his pillow at her next visit. Damian recovers the next day, grooms himself with care to please May, and returns to January's service meekly, behaving so nicely that everyone speaks well of him.

The narrator's heavy **irony** continues as he offers the opinion that May's decision to become Damian's lover represents the kind of 'generosity' women are capable of when they act without consultation (see Themes, on Anti-Feminism). A harder heart, and the implication is that this is his own position, would have preferred to see the young sexual predator drop dead. May's actions are again pragmatic: her letter is not in verse, but comes straight to the point and is effectively delivered. The gesture with which it is thrust under Damian's pillow and his hand is squeezed is assertive and can be read as a sexual **metaphor**, indicating that despite convention and appearance, it is the woman who is in charge.

In this suggested role-reversal, Damian now gives himself up to preening. Hitherto he has been presented as a relatively neutral victim of May's charms; now he takes on the character of the deceiving dissembler, like the adder in Eden with whom he has been compared already. His hypocrisy with January and the other members of the household ensures that he continues to be trusted.

All pretence that this is a story of true love is now stripped away in preparation for the tale's sordid conclusion. Chaucer's construction of the Merchant narrator's voice continues to assert itself dramatically as the **tone** becomes more direct and embittered, the irony more corrosive.

- *776* **narwe** carefully
- *778* **stoon** stoon
- *781* **sterven** die (i.e. of unrequited love)
- *781* **cruell pride** cold haughtiness
- *782* **homicide** murder
- *786* **There lakketh noght** nothing is wanting
- *787* **unto his lust suffise** satisfy his desires
- *788* **wole devise** wishes to contrive things
- *791* **threste** thrust
- *792* **pilwe** pillow
- *794* **harde him twiste** squeezed (his hand) hard
- *799* **kembeth him** combs himself
  preyneth him preens himself
  piketh picks himself over, grooms himself
- *801* **as lowe** as humbly
- *802* **a dogge for the bowe** a dog out hunting with an archer
- *804* **(For craft is al, whoso that do it kan)** for cunning is everything for those who know how to pull it off

LINES 809—44   January makes a garden for himself and May

Scholars say that happiness lies in sensuous pleasure, and January is determined to surround himself with nice things appropriate to his social position.
He makes a walled garden, so beautiful that legendary gardens hardly
compare, and the gods themselves choose to play there. January keeps the
gate locked and kept the key to himself, so that he and May can go there to
make love in the summertime. But earthly pleasure can be short-lived…

> January follows the teaching of Epicurus, the ancient Roman scholar
> whose philosophy was popularly interpreted as suggesting that pleasure
> should be the main goal in life. January's sensuous indulgences are
> fitting for his station, however, in a period in which 'Sumptuary Laws'
> carefully laid down, for example, which ranks in society were permitted
> to wear which fabrics and furs (designed to prevent new mercantile
> wealth presuming to take on the ceremonial garments the aristocracy
> reserved for themselves).
>
> The garden which January constructs reminds the attentive reader of
> earlier references to Adam and Eve, although the other gardens with
> which it is compared here are all in classical mythology or secular
> **romance**. This garden is a **parody** of Eden from the outset, as Adam
> and Eve became self-consciously sexual beings only after they were
> expelled from Eden, whereas January's garden is devised as a place in
> which he and May can add variety to their sex life.
>
> Sexual **imagery** abounds, as Priapus, the pagan god of gardens, is also
> the god of the phallus. Keys and keyholes are also commonly metaphors
> for sex, as will become more explicitly evident later. Given the
> astrological imagery also associated with January and May (see
> Themes, on Calendars and Astrology) it is clear that January is in
> danger: summertime is May's season, and the outdoor world is her
> sphere of influence, whereas January's sphere of influence is indoors.
>
> The passage bears comparison with the earlier description of the
> wedding feast, but where January dominated there, on this occasion
> the initiative lies with May.

810 **Stant in delit** lies in sensual pleasure

813 **Shoop him** contrived, managed
814 **as honestly to his degree** as suitably as his rank dictated
820 **the Romance of the Rose** (a long French **allegorical romance**, written by Guillaume de Loris and continued by Jean de Meun and translated into English in part by Chaucer. In the poem the **protagonist**-lover seeks a perfect rose)
826 **Pluto and his queene Proserpina** Pluto and Proserpine his queen (classical divinities of the underworld, appropriated in medieval British tradition as king and queen of the fairies)
833 **wiket** wicket-gate
835 **cliket** latchkey
835 **unshette** unlocked
836 **paye his wyf her dette** have sexual relations with his wife (in a manner proper to married couples)
840 **spedde** thrived, succeeded
843 **dure** endure, last

LINES 845–84   Suddenly January goes blind

What very bad luck. Fortune is just like the scorpion which smiles with its face while it stings you with its poisonous tail. Just as January is deceived into believing he has found stable happiness he suddenly goes blind. He weeps and wants to die because he thinks he will lose his wife, whereas he wants her to be faithful to him even after his death. Eventually he becomes reconciled to his blindness except that he remains so jealous that he will not let May out of his clutches. This makes her weep and want to die because she is in love with Damian.

For the second time (see lines 571–79) Chaucer uses the device of **apostrophe**, combined with **hyperbole** for comic effect. January goes suddenly blind. At the narrative level this turn in the plot is quite arbitrary. The tale's meaning is, however, carried largely at the level of **metaphor** and **image** and in this respect January's physical blindness is a fulfilment of the metaphorical blindness of self-delusion which has afflicted him from the outset (see Language and Style, on Imagery). At line 386 the reader has been reminded of the **proverb** 'love is blind', and January's character has been built up to this point as a demonstration of the truth of the saying.

A further metaphor in the passage picks up on another theme and major field of imagery in the tale (see Themes, on Calendars and Astrology), when fortune is compared to the scorpion. In Chaucer's time it was understood that different signs of the zodiac ruled different parts of the body: Scorpio, symbolised by a scorpion with its tail erect ready to strike, governed the male genitals. The implication here is that January's misfortune has a sexual dimension to it, that while fortune has apparently been smiling on him, all the time it has held a threat, and that threat, as everyone except January already knows, is sexual. Accordingly, while Damian has not hitherto been incorporated into the binary astrological opposition between January and May, he now takes his place within that metaphorical scheme by implication.

Fortune is **personified** in the passage, as is common in Chaucer's writing. Like a number of abstract qualities which have female **grammatical gender** in Latin, the personification is feminised, and she is presented as a woman, often blindfold, to demonstrate the arbitrariness of her operation, and holding a wheel on which her victims rise and fall. Fortune is closely associated with the moon, signifying changeability (see lines 673 and following). Changeability is indicated in this passage by a high incidence of **antitheses,** such as line 846, and **oxymorons** such as 'brotil joye' and 'sweete venym' (line 849).

845   **sodeyn hap** sudden occurrence
846   **deceyvable** deceitful
848   **envenyminge** poisoning
849   **queynte** ingenious, curious
850   **peynte** paint, portray
851   **hewe** disguise, complexion
      stidefastnesse steadfastness, constancy
855   **biraft** deprived of, taken away from
      yen eyes
856   **dien** die
859   **woxen** grown
867   **widwe** widow
868   **Soul** alone, solo
870   **aswage** diminish, soothe

874 **everemoore in oon** continuously
875 **outrageous** excessive
879 **hond** hand
881 **beningnely** tenderly
884 **breste** burst, break

LINES 885–919 Love conquers all

Damian is also miserable because he cannot spend time alone with May. Nonetheless, by writing to each other and by silent signals, they understand each other. In fact it would make little difference to January if he could see. May has made a wax impression of the key to the garden gate for Damian, who makes a secret copy of the key. Something wonderful will happen as a result. Love always finds a way...

In preparation for the conclusion of the plot, two of the main **metaphors** which have been threaded through the tale are now brought to explicit conclusion. The narrator philosophises on different types of blindness and the relative importance of foresight and judgement as against physical sight. Many people, he concludes, are blind without knowing it. The **images** of impressionability which have also occurred earlier in the tale are now fulfilled through the device of **traductio** as May physically makes an imprint of the key to the garden in warm wax. Previously January had hoped to mould her like wax (line 218), whereas it was Damian who made an instant impression on her (line 766).

The choice of 'privee' (line 893) to describe the signals passed between the two lovers provides an unfortunate **pun** for comic effect, as it reminds the reader of the fate of Damian's love-letter, thrown down the privy (line 742), and the basic nature of Damian and May's attractions and ambitions. This is incongruously compared yet again with noble examples taken from classical legend, as January is ludicrously paired with Argus, a giant with a hundred eyes. Damian and May are identified with Pyramus and Thisbe, the lovers who eloped after speaking to each other through a chink in a wall. Shakespeare was later to turn their tragedy to comic effect in *A Midsummer's Night's Dream*. These, like other classical references sprinkled through the tale, are drawn from the Latin poet Ovid, considered in Chaucer's time to be the major classical poet of love.

The tone of the passage, as elsewhere, is a dramatisation of the narrator's jaded attitude to love, where all the old **aphorisms** and **clichés**, 'love is blind', 'love conquers all', 'love will find a way', 'the course of true love never did run smooth', are implied and **ironically** dismissed. The tale suggests that all the great literature of love is empty nonsense, more likely to delude the reader than illuminate the subject, as real relationships are driven by sexual desire alone.

889 **purpos** intentions
890 **But if that** unless, except
893 **privee signes** secret signals
894 **the fin** end, conclusion
896 **fer** far
900 **poure** look closely, pore
       pryen peer, pry
902 **wenen** believes
903 **an ese** a comfort, relief
904 **yoore** long ago
909 **countrefeted** copied
913 **seystou** you say
914 **sleighte** cunning trick, plan
916 **Piramus and Tesbee** Pyramus and Thisbe
917 **streite** strictly
918 **rowninge** whispering

LINES 920–72   **While January reaffirms his marriage vows, Damian slips into the garden**

Eight days before the end of May, January develops a desire to take his wife into the garden. He persuades her in the ignorant language lovers have always used. She signals to Damian to go before them through the gate, which he does, hiding under a bush to wait for her. Blind old January leads May into the garden and slams the gate. Before commencing his lovemaking, he reaffirms his marriage vows, reminding her of the three benefits marriage to him confers on her, despite his unattractiveness, and asks her for a kiss.

Confirmation of the attitude of disillusion, which characterises the narrative voice in *The Merchant's Tale,* is the description of January's address to May as 'olde lewed wordes' (line 937); in fact the words are drawn closely, if inappropriately, from the Bible. The Song of Solomon, also known as *Song of Songs* or *Canticles,* is a lyrical love song in the Old Testament, interpreted by the Jewish faith as an expression of love by God for his chosen people, and by Christianity as a **metaphor** for Christ's relationship with his spouse the Church.

The comic effect of this passage is achieved through **bathos**, as January's words are immediately followed by the detail, with its unavoidable sexual innuendo, of Damian's unlocking the gate, sneaking into the garden and sitting under a bush. January's slamming of the gate anticipates his sudden interruption of the later lovemaking. January's second address to May, once they are in the garden, offers a reprise of their marriage vows, sealed with a kiss, but this time undertaken at a season and in a place more auspicious to May (see Themes, on Calendars and Astrology). January says that 'winter is goon' (line 928), ironically anticipating his own imminent dismissal. It is also his turn to take up the imprinting metaphor: such is the impression made by May's beauty that he can still see her despite his blindness. But the **image** is now irrevocably tarnished by connotations of deceitfulness and faking, since the episode of the copying of the key.

January offers May three things to compensate for being married to a blind old man: the benefit to her soul of the married condition, the social position it confers, and, last but not least, all his wealth with which he now gives her a free hand. It is worth considering how the passage works **tonally**, particularly whether expressions like 'verray love' (line 971) convey the idea that January really does now love May, with all the **pathos** that implies in the circumstances, or whether the pervasive cynicism of the narrative voice prevents the reader from finding any character capable of altruism.

920 **to purpos** to the point
922 **caught so greet a wil** developed a great desire
923 **egging** urging, encouraging (as in 'egging on')
927 **turtles vois** the song of the turtle dove (noted for sexual fidelity)

928   **reynes weete** wet rain

929   **columbin** like a dove's

934   **spot** (moral) stain, blemish

935   **disport** relaxation, entertainment

937   **lewed** ignorant, stupid, worthless

941   **stirte** started, leapt

947   **clapte** slammed

951   **Levere** rather

961   **chartres** legally binding documents

965   **wite** blame, reproach

966   **depe enprented** deeply imprinted

968   **unlikly** unlovely

972   **rome aboute** stroll around

LINES $973-1006$ **May promises to be true to January while signalling to Damian**

May responds to January firstly by bursting into tears, then reminding him that she has an immortal soul to look after just as he does, as well as womanly honour, which she placed in his hands when she took her marriage vows before the priest. If she should ever bring shame on her family, may she be tied in a sack and thrown in the nearest river. Men are always unjustly suspicious of women. At that moment she spots Damian in the bush and signals to him to climb a fruit tree. He immediately does so, as she has already described what to do in a letter and he understands her perfectly.

> May's hypocrisy in this passage is audacious. She pays lip-service to the moral teaching of medieval Christianity, which condemns the unfaithful wife to hell, while simultaneously setting the stage for her own sexual infidelity. Her assertion that men are always accusing women of infidelity is borne out by the subject of this tale and its anti-feminist precursors (see Themes, on Anti-Feminism). Like Chaucer's Wife of Bath, she complains about the way women are stereotyped while simultaneously acting out the stereotype. Her melodramatic suggestion that if she is unfaithful she should be stripped, put in a sack and thrown in the river, while adding to the comic **irony** of the passage, can be read as the narrator's fervent wish for all unfaithful women.

The narrator does not describe the signs she and Damian make to each other, but the detail that she used her finger is sexually suggestive. The fact that the tree he climbs is full of fruit has a number of connotations. Fruit **imagery** is frequently associated with sex, particularly the pear tree, which features in lewd popular anonymous lyric verses of the period as well as in one of the stories in *The Decameron* by Chaucer's Italian contemporary Giovanni Boccaccio. May calls her wifehood a tender flower, but the passage indicates by **metonymy** that she is less a flower than a ripe fruit.

More specifically, however, this passage fulfils the biblical theme which was set up earlier (see Themes, on Joseph and Mary / Adam and Eve). The garden is a **parody** of the Garden of Eden, with the devil in the guise of an adder hiding in a fruit tree tempting Eve to eat the fruit of knowledge and learn the nature of good and evil (see lines 530–82). Damian is the tempter, although in this instance arguably May has been setting the pace. She already knows the difference between good and evil but chooses to ignore the information in her quest for sexual gratification.

975   **forward** foremost

978   **thilke tendre flour** that same fragile flower

979   **assured** pledged, entrusted

986   **empeyre** damage, impair

988   **strepe** strip

989   **drenche** drown

992   **have repreve of** are reproached by

      ay newe constantly, continuously

993   **contenance** expression

999   **charged** laden, full

1004   **how he werchen shal** how he must behave, what he must do

1005   **pyrie** pear tree

LINES $1007-63$ **A digression concerning the king and queen of fairyland**

It was a lovely sunny morning at the end of May. The king and queen of fairies, with a number of the queen's attendants, are present at the other side of the garden. Pluto, the king, expresses outrage to his wife about May's behaviour, which he sees as typical of a woman, and undertakes to restore January's sight so that he can find out what his May is up to. Queen Proserpine retaliates by promising to give all women caught red-handed the persuasive powers to run rings around their husbands.

> The whole purpose of this passage is to create suspense, and its elaborate **circumlocution** pushes the possibilities to their limits. Firstly a sunny morning is embellished with **personification** and astrological detail. Then the reader learns that the garden is quite crowded: January, May and Damian have an audience of fairies. There is some danger of a digression within the digression, as the mythological history of the marriage of the king and queen of fairies, in their original guise as king and queen of the pagan Underworld, is alluded to, but the narrator contents himself with supplying bibliographical references for those who wish to follow up this line of enquiry.
>
> The **style** of the passage **parodies** the opening of romance narrative, where it would set an elevated **tone** and provide the author with an opportunity to display his erudite credentials; here it is a comic delaying tactic. Pluto subscribes to the same anti-feminist propaganda that all the mortal males in the tale believe (see Themes, on Anti-Feminism) and cites learned authorities from the Bible in support of his case. He immediately becomes January's champion, promising to restore his eyesight. Proserpine, in protection of women, ensures that although his physical sight may be restored, he, and all men, will be just as **metaphorically** blind to their wives' true nature as they have always been. That the king and queen of fairies are also having a domestic debate about marital fidelity, suggests that the battle of the sexes is universal, and not confined to mere mortals.

1007   **blew the firmament** blue the sky

1008   **Phebus** Phoebus (the sun)

       stremes beams

1011   **But litel fro his declinacion** about to move into the descendant (i.e. of waning influence)

1012   **Jovis exaltacion** with Jupiter at its strongest influence

1013   **morwe-tide** morning

1014 **in the ferther side** at the far side

1018 **Which that he ravisshed out of Ethna** whom he carried off from Etna by force

1020 **Claudian** Claudius Claudianus (fourth-century Latin author of *De Raptu Proserpinae* [The Rape of Prosperpine])

1021 **grisely** grim, hideous

    fette fetched

1025 **ther may no wight seye nay** no one may deny it

1026 **preveth** proves

1027 **tresons** betrayals

1030 **Salomon** Solomon (Old Testament king noted for wisdom and for having many wives)

1031 **Fulfild of sapience** replete with wisdom

1033 **wit and reson kan** is equipped with sense and the power of reason

1034 **bountee** goodness, kindness

1036 **noon** not one

1038 ***filius Syrak*** son of Syrak (Latin. Jesus son of Syrak reputedly wrote the Apocryphal Book of Ecclesiasticus)

1039 **Ne speketh of yow but seelde reverence** seldom speaks of you with respect

1040 **corrupt pestilence** foul plague

1046 **of my magestee** by the power vested in me

1048 **ayen** again, once more

1049 **wold doon him vileyneye** wants to do harm to him (i.e. betray him)

1050 **harlotrye** loose living

1051 **Bothe in repreve of hire and othere mo** both to reproach her and others as well

1053 **my moodres sires soule** the soul of my mother's father (in this case Saturn)

1054 **suffisant** adequate

1058 **bere hem doun** bear down upon them, overthrow them

1060 **Al had man seyn** even if a man has seen

1061 **visage it hardily** face it out boldly

LINES $1064–1107$ **Prosperine argues the woman's case with vigour**

Proserpine makes it clear that she is not impressed by the learned authorities cited by Pluto, particularly Solomon, who, she points out, has a dubious reputation anyway since he turned his back on God late in life and had a reputation for sexual excess. She becomes increasingly heated, citing all the female saints and the Roman female martyrs too. She will never

Y

refrain from criticising Solomon for being so critical. Pluto concedes the argument but insists on restoring January's sight. Proserpine agrees to contradict him no more, but to provide May with a ready explanation for her behaviour.

The voice of Proserpine is dramatised so that she sounds less and less like a fairy and suspiciously like the Wife of Bath. She, too, rejected learned authority in favour of the testimony of experience. The **irony** of the passage lies in the fact that Proserpine becomes heated because Solomon accuses women of excessive chattering, which is precisely what she is doing. Lines 1079 to 1090, in particular, with their torrent of **rhetorical questions** represent a hectoring style of argument, and her expletives are extremely colourful. Moreover, she promises to supply May and all women with the strength of argument to have the last word, which is what she succeeds in doing, as Pluto gives in.

Pluto, on the other hand, is given the voice of a weary husband who will do anything for a quiet life. Accordingly, comic effect is once more achieved by the contrast between style and dramatic circumstance. On numerous occasions earlier in the tale, the language of religion, scholarship and **courtly love** is used in relatively trivial and homely contexts, whereas here, when the tale finally does report on the **discourse** of supernatural beings, they are having a stereotypical domestic squabble. The material about Solomon that Prosperpine cites is drawn from the Old Testament, I Kings 11. During the debate between Pluto and Proserpine the narrative voice and attitude which is associated with the dramatised character of the Merchant recedes; the stylistic games in this passage appear to come unmediated from Chaucer.

1064 **What rekketh me** What does it matter to me? What do I care?

1070 **in Cristes hous** in heaven (i.e. female saints and martyrs)

1071 **hey preved hire constance** they proved their fidelity, constancy

1072 **geestes** historical stories

1076 **the sentence** sense, meaning

1077 **sovereyn bontee** supreme goodness

1083 **false goddis** pagan idols

1084 **forbode** forbidden

1085 **emplastre** gloss over

1086 **idolastre** idolater

1090 **rather than he wolde** sooner than he wanted

1092 **boterflye** butterfly

1095 **jangleresses** chatterers, gossips

1096 **I moote brouke my tresses** I am able to keep my hair

1104 **sit** is fitting

1108 **contrarie** contradict

LINES 1108–41   May and Damian make love in a tree

Returning to January, we find him wandering the paths of the garden with May and singing love songs. Eventually they get back to the pear tree where Damian is hiding. May tells January that, because of her condition, she has a craving for pears. January regrets that he does not have a servant to hand who can climb as he is blind. She suggests that he embrace the trunk of the tree, so that she can climb on his back. He willingly agrees and bends down. May climbs into the tree, Damian lifts her smock and thrusts himself in.

See Extended Commentaries, Text 3

1110 **papejay** parrot

1112 **aleyes** paths, alleys

1122 **for hir love that is of hevene queene** for the love of the Queen of Heaven (i.e. the Virgin Mary)

1123 **in my plit** in my predicament, condition, state

1128 **no fors** it is not a problem

1129 **vouche sauf** grant, agree

1135 **myn herte blood** life-blood

1137 **caughte hire by a twiste** caught hold of a branch

1139 **glose** gloss over it, use circumlocution

1141 **throng** thrust

LINES 1142–1206   January regains his sight and cannot believe his eyes

Pluto, outraged at what May is doing, restores January's sight; January looks up and cries out at what he sees. May claims that she had been taught that struggling with a man in a tree would restore his sight. January disputes the nature of the struggle, but May retorts that if he indeed thinks he saw her having sex with Damian her medicine has not worked and his sight is still faulty. He apologises, and she warns him that someone whose sight has just been restored, like someone newly wakened, may begin by misjudging what they see and it will be that way for some days. She then jumps out of the tree, he kisses and hugs her, strokes her belly and takes her home to the palace, and that is the end of the story.

> In the final **denouement** of the plot, the far-fetchedness of what is going on provides a comic parallel to January's gullibility, which seems to know no bounds. Humour derives from the imagined physical circumstances in which the debate takes place, from the improbability of May's argument, and from old January's womanish wailing. Chaucer's woefully inappropriate simile, comparing January to a woman whose child has died, is not only terminally unsexing for him, but a gloriously incongruous literary reference. In medieval biblical plays, such as the mystery plays, one of the most dramatic moments occurs with the lamentations of the mothers of the baby boys murdered by Herod's soldiers. In such plays, all the female parts are played by men, and the implications of the reference are that January is both womanish and over-dramatic in his response. Damian, on the other hand, is reduced to a phallus in a pear tree, a mechanical function of the plot.
>
> May is in full control at the end of the story, with her supernaturally-assisted presence of mind in the circumstances, and her vigorous and unladylike leap down from the tree. Yet there are a number of ways in which the ending of the tale varies from the common **fabliau** conclusion in which the whole edifice of deceit comes tumbling down, and the characters are allowed no possibility of an afterlife. Throughout *The Merchant's Tale* there have been suggestions that a serious lesson may be drawn from the particular case, albeit a wholly negative one, and that this is more than a farcical romp.
>
> Accordingly, the final paragraphs contain hints of foreboding for the future. May warns January that his eyes may go on deceiving him, suggesting that discovery has not cut off the means for her

relationship with Damian to continue. January strokes her womb, picking up on the earlier hint at line 1123 that she is pregnant. The reader is left to wonder if she was when she claimed to crave pears, or if she is now, and if she turns out to be, who will inherit old January's wealth, which is the anxiety with which the tale began. Note that the passage has moved from the present to the past tense in preparation for withdrawal from the story, and that the Merchant's apologies for using blunt language draw attention to it (see further Language and Style).

1149 **dressed** treated

1151 **But if** unless

1151 **uncurteisly** rudely, discourteously

1152 **yaf** gave

1154 **harrow** (expletive expressing dismay)

1155 **stoore** bold, brazen

1159 **Up peril** on the fate of

1164 **algate** at any rate, nevertheless

1166 **swived** fucked

1171 **glimsing** glimpsing, squinting

1179 **lief** dear

missaid spoken out of turn

1180 **I am yvele apaid** I am upset, seriously dissatisfied

1181 **I wende han seyn** I believed I had seen

1182 **by thee leyn** lain with you (**euphemism** for having sex)

1186 **taken keep** take notice, attend to

1188 **adawed** aroused

1190 **yse** see

1193 **ysatled** settled

1194 **bigile** deceive

1198 **misconceyveth** misunderstands

misdemeth misjudges

1201 **clippeth** embraces

y

LINES $1207-1228$ **Harry Bailey responds by confiding that his wife is by no means perfect either**

The Host hopes to be preserved from a wife like May. All women are full of tricks to deceive men, however, as *The Merchant's Tale* proves. He himself has a wife, who, though poor, has a number of vices. He regrets he ever married her, and would tell the company why except that it would be bound to get back to her, so he resolves to let the matter go.

> The Host can always be relied upon to respond in an enthusiastic but simplistic way to the material of each tale. The inadequacy of his responses directs the reader towards the literary and philosophical complexities that he misses. On this occasion, his is a knee-jerk anti-feminist response to the superficial level of the plot, and a corroboration of the Merchant's narratorial position, which ignores the wider allegorical and mythical dimensions of the tale (see Themes). His description of his own wife, so far as it goes, is in many respects a cruder example of anti-feminism than the Merchant's own. One word, 'chaffare' (line 1226) does, however encode the wider themes associated with Chaucer's satire of mercantile values, as it suggests **metaphorically** that problems arise with relations between the sexes when the values of religion and romance are put on one side and everything is seen as a matter of business or trade.

1209   **sleightes** tricks

1211   **sely** innocent, naive

1212   **soothe** truth

      weyve weave, wander

1215   **povre** poor

1216   **a labbing shrewe** a blabbing scold

1219   **In conseil** in confidence

1220   **Me reweth soore** it is a great regret to me

1221   **rekenen** count, enumerate

1222   **nice** foolish

1226   **konnen outen swich chaffare** know how to display such business

PART THREE

CRITICAL APPROACHES

CHARACTERISATION

In a layered narrative like *The Canterbury Tales,* characterisation is a complex matter. Characters within *The Merchant's Tale* fulfil the functions required of them by the plot and, as with any story in which the participants are going to be the objects of ridicule, they are animated just enough to appear plausible, but do not develop the kind of complex inner life which would cause the audience to sympathise with them too much.

The complications arise, however, when we consider who is the creator of January, May and Damian, for the Merchant is a fictional character, too. He exists at a different layer in the narrative composition, but is given physical characteristics both in the *General Prologue* and in the introduction to his tale. It is Chaucer's creation of the Merchant's voice to which we are supposed to be listening. Chaucer himself, however, is part of the fiction, for he has put himself on the pilgrimage, and pretends that the retelling of each story is a prodigious feat of memory. In a modern novel, the inner thoughts of characters can provide the reader with a lens through which to see the world the characters inhabit; in *The Merchant's Tale* understanding the function of character is about being alert to a series of lenses through which we are offered a picture of a dysfunctional marriage.

CHAUCER THE VENTRILOQUIST

Chaucer's characterisation of himself is the complicating factor which prevents the pilgrims in *The Canterbury Tales* from being read like characters in a play. Chaucer puts himself on the pilgrimage, and attempts twice to tell stories in his own voice with disastrous results – *Melibee* and *Sir Thopas* are both experiments in bad story-telling. The whole, completely fictitious, retelling of the pilgrims' stories is presented as a diligent feat of memory on Chaucer's part. His caricature of himself as a timid and inept inventor of stories allows him to suggest that he is not competent to sift the good from the bad in what he has heard, so he must retell it all.

From this position he is able to tell an explicit story about illicit sex by hiding behind the character of the Merchant. Chaucer implies that he cannot control the Merchant, although of course the Merchant is his own invention. Thus Chaucer uses the character of the Merchant to give himself the freedom to tell a tale about sex. But equally he does not necessarily imply that he agrees with the attitude he has thereby constructed. He intervenes in his own voice at the end of *The Clerk's Tale*, urging women not to behave passively in the face of husbands who make unreasonable demands on them. This may suggest to the reader that the Merchant's presentation of bad marriages as being the fault of bad wives is not a view to which Chaucer himself subscribes. It certainly sets the scene for different possible readings of what is to follow.

THE MERCHANT

The characterisation of Chaucer's Merchant has given rise to extensive critical debate, not helped by the dubious status of the Merchant's *Prologue* which does not exist in many of the manuscripts of *The Canterbury Tales*. The debate begins by considering whether or not the portrait in the *General Prologue* is sympathetic. Is he vain or is he successful? Is he hypocritical or is he just a man of the world? Is the Merchant's *Prologue* the outpouring of an embittered man, or the humorous exaggeration of a newly-married man away from his wife for the first time in predominantly male company? Perhaps one way of reconciling the possibilities is to acknowledge that there are fundamentally **paradoxical** elements to the character: he talks openly and at length about business, including revealing that he is involved in illegal currency-dealing, yet does not reveal his name or financial status. In his tale, too, he is at times very oblique in the expression of opinion, yet is also capable of shocking frankness. The Merchant, like all the pilgrims, apparently manipulates an old story to his own purposes. The implication is that this tale about one bad marriage is a tale about all marriages but particularly his own, though the reader looking for evidence to support such an assumption will be hard put to find any. Within the tale itself, the Merchant appears to direct the reader towards seeing January as misguided from the outset; to understanding that the sacrament is a sham designed to lend respectability to motives which are wholly about materialism and sexual desire; that all women are devious and lecherous like May, and that January's garden project is a joke. Chaucer leaves room, however, for the reader to reject this interpretation and observe that all the obscenities in the tale are the narrator's. He invites the reader to consider the possibility that January actually believes in what he is doing, wants to do what is right within the conventions of the time, is sincere in his Christian belief and is actually in love with May. These two possible readings of the tale also accommodate the two interpretations of the Merchant as either an embittered and disillusioned man with an unhealthy interest in sex, or an urbane man of the world who, with tongue firmly in cheek, is caricaturing himself not only in the *Prologue* to his tale but in the attitude Chaucer has him strike as a narrator.

THE CHARACTERS OF THE TALE

A number of factors come together to distance the reader from the characters of the tale, not least the complicated and ambiguous series of lenses through which they are viewed. They are all types or **allegories** to lesser or greater degrees. January is the only character who is allowed to develop anything approaching an inner life, and there should be enough in all the reported thoughts and speeches given to him in the first half of the tale to allow a sense of an individual intelligence to form. Yet the narrator's attitude intervenes so much that January is never allowed to become more than a pitiful case-study, his every word, thought and move mediated by a voice which is inherently opposed to his views and engaged in mocking him (see Language and Style on Speech). The characterisation of January also owes much to convention, in his case the *senex amans* (old-man lover) **burlesque** character of anti-feminist literature (see Themes on Anti-Feminism). The same is true of Damian, for, although he suffers terrible love-sickness, it is described in wholly conventional terms, so he never develops as an individual. Once May has provided the means by which he recovers, he becomes simply a function in the plot, so that the reader barely notices that he has been left up the pear tree when the story ends. Damian is the real wax character, so impressed by May that he cannot function, then entirely at her beck and call.

May is characterised largely by what is not said of her. We do not know why she marries January in the first place and are not even prompted to ask. What she thinks of his love-making we *are* prompted to ask, but the

Y

question goes unanswered on more than one occasion (see lines 639–40, 749, 752). She becomes Damian's lover out of pity, but line 774:

> Lo, pitee renneth soone in gentil herte

is Chaucer's favourite, occurring in *The Knight's Tale, The Squire's Tale* and *The Legend of Good Women*, and is perhaps least convincing here as May is not 'gentil'. The reader is left to surmise whether the line is **ironic**, but any assumption that May is simply sex-mad has no positive foundation in the text, either. She is very active, and appears to embrace the pear tree project with some vigour, yet she also does everything January asks of her without complaint and there is nowhere any hint that she dislikes or is repelled by him.

The other characters in the tale are either **personification allegories** or mythical beings. Placebo and Justinus, representing the abstract properties of good and bad advice, are drawn from court **satire** and contemporary advice literature in which the recipient, usually a prince, is told how to choose good counsellors and to avoid flatterers whose motive is the advancement of their own careers. This element in the tale may have some topical resonance for Chaucer's original audience, as the king at the time, Richard II, notoriously surrounded himself with self-seeking young favourites against the advice of the elder statesmen at court (see Background). Pluto and Proserpine are the characters arguably imbued with most personality, or at least with the most believable relationship, and they are not human beings at all.

THEMES

MARRIAGE

In Chaucer's day, real life marriage was rarely undertaken for love, and was least likely to be so among the upper classes where consolidation of title, land and money was paramount. Hence betrothals of infants were common, as was marriage between young girls and elderly men in search of male heirs. Chaucer's own granddaughter, Alice, was first married in her early teens to a man in his fifties. She was to outlive him and two other husbands and bear only one child, a son, to the third husband. Once married, a woman had the same legal status as her husband's domestic animals, so the equation made in *The Merchant's Tale* (lines 99–102) is not that shocking in context. A treatise known as *The Goodman of Paris*, written by a benign elderly husband for his young wife, instructing her on how she might improve her wifely conduct in her next marriage, suggests that she observe his lap-dog and copy its behaviour, keeping close to the man who provides her with food and shelter, even if he maltreats her. She must be like the dog on the road, at table and in bed. It is important to remember in reading the tale that it was not uncommon to 'buy' a bride. In particular, there was traffic between wealthy urban merchants using their money to seek country estates, coats of arms and the status at court that went with those things, by marrying their sons and daughters off to the offspring of impoverished members of the landed classes. Conventional attitudes to the institution of marriage were, in all seriousness, very close to January's, and the presentation of marriage as a mercantile transaction, although it offers opportunities for **satire** in a tale told by a Merchant, represents an actuality. Marriage was, and is, however, also a sacrament of the Church, and here the picture presented in *The Merchant's Tale* is less neutral. The sacrament involves the exchange of vows of care and fidelity, sanctifying the partnership in the eyes of God. Where those vows are kept, as they eventually are in *The Franklin's Tale*, the marriage may be said to be good, despite the inequality of the partners. The embittered narrator of *The Merchant's Tale*, however, draws no distinction between good and bad marriage and belittles the sacrament itself.

ANTI-FEMINISM

St Jerome, the translator of the Vulgate Latin Bible, was the ultimate authority on women in the Middle Ages. His was the first and most influential pronouncement on the celibacy of the clergy. He was adamant, and cited the Bible to support his views, that virginity was far superior to the married state. Marriage was, at best, a necessary evil. Jerome also quoted one pagan authority called Theophrastus, whose work does not survive, but who is believed to have written a short vitriolic treatise containing the archetypal portrait of a wicked wife. Then a twelfth-century British writer, Walter Map, wrote a long commentary in the form of a letter to a friend, citing mythical and biblical reasons why he should not marry. With that, a literary tradition of misogynist writing was established.

The voice given to Chaucer's Merchant lies squarely within this tradition, and the Wife of Bath is designed as a living example of the kind of wife warned against in the treatises. Aspects of the mercantile **imagery** January employs, to describe the young wife he sets out to acquire, compare women with food. The older woman is conventionally described as left-overs, the 'forage' (line 210) or animal food that remains when the best of the harvest has gone. The Wife of Bath, in the *Prologue* to her tale, colludes in this devaluing of the mature woman, when she says that as the 'flour' is gone, she must sell the 'bran' as best she can (lines 477–78). Chaucer's art is, in fact, unusual, in that it leaves some room for the reader to develop sympathy for the woman's case.

Eustace Deschamps, Chaucer's French contemporary, is remembered for his long and partisan *Miroir de Mariage* ('Mirror of Marriage') which includes a list of the ploys used by a woman when her husband will not give her what she wants, on how she will deceive him, and on how everything in marriage turns to torment for the man, whether his wife is beautiful or ugly, rich or poor. Texts written within this tradition came to be known generically as *'mal marié'* ('badly married') and evolve into conventional diatribes in which the speaker, a man, simply lists his wife's failings. One woman, again a French contemporary of Chaucer's, Christine de Pisan, wrote a rejoinder. Her *Épistre du Dieu d'Amours* ('Letter to Cupid') scathingly points out the discrepancy between the literary romance convention of **courtly love** in which men languish and threaten to die from unrequited love for unattainable women, and the wide-spread male assertion in the anti-feminist tradition that women are inferior beings who are not worth having anyway.

JOSEPH AND MARY / ADAM AND EVE

The problem for women in a world dominated by Christian theology interpreted by celibate male writers, was twofold. First there was the legacy of Eve, the first woman, who was given to Adam as a help and companion. She was beguiled by the devil disguised as an adder, in the Garden of Eden, into eating the forbidden fruit and was, therefore, blamed for the loss of Paradise. **Ironic** references to the story from Genesis 2 abound in *The Merchant's Tale*. Early in the tale, when the narrator is extolling the supposed virtues of marriage, he cites the story in support of his argument (lines 113–17). The later events in January's garden are primarily a

burlesque, which derives much of its meaning from a knowledge of the Genesis story. May and Damian, the latter previously described as an adder (line 574), finally betray January in the fruit tree in the garden, although in this case the garden has been designed for sexual pleasure from the outset, and it is May who has led the way in devising the betrayal.

Secondly, women had to deal with the role-model of the Virgin Mary, cited by theologians as the woman who reversed the pattern of Eve, who was, in being both virgin and mother, an impossible act to follow biologically. The story of Mary's betrothal to the old Joseph is also threaded through the tale, and January and May even share the same initials. That story is itself complicated by accretions in the **apocryphal Gospels** of the Nativity, *Pseudo-Matthew* and *The Protevangelium*, which embellish it with accounts of the early life of the Virgin. According to the full story as it was understood in Chaucer's time, old Joseph presented himself at the temple as an unwilling suitor for Mary, but the rod he carried suddenly and miraculously burst into bloom, a sign that he was God's chosen husband for her. January is not an unwilling suitor, but describes himself as a tree miraculously blooming in his old age (lines 249–50). The story of the Virgin Birth – found in Matthew 1:19–20 but much embellished in the Apocrypha – was also commonly incorporated into comic anti-feminist stories. When Joseph returned and found Mary pregnant, he was first minded not to believe her account of the angel's visit and to abandon her, and his doubts had to be corrected by an angel. **Fabliaux** abound in which either gullible girls are persuaded into adultery with men dressed up as angels, or gullible husbands returning from a period of absence are persuaded that their wives' unexpected pregnancies are of supernatural origin. In *The Merchant's Tale*, January is offered an implausible explanation of what was happening in the pear tree. He is persuaded to believe because of the intervention of Proserpine, the pagan goddess of, among other things, women in childbirth. When he strokes May's womb (line 1202), January, like Joseph, is happily reconciled with a woman who is bearing a child that is not his.

CALENDARS AND ASTROLOGY

The names of the principal characters in *The Merchant's Tale* indicate that they are types rather than individuals. The tale develops a calendrial theme, suggesting that winter should not attempt to marry early summer. The tale is, moreover, embellished with precise astrological references which take it beyond the bounds of simple **fabliau**. Medieval calendars were elaborate things, showing all the fixed and movable feasts of the Church, traditional human occupations for the month, and a star-chart showing the zodiac – for astrology was, for Chaucer and his contemporaries, part of mainstream scientific learning. January is the season of feasting, marked by images of an old man toasting his feet by a roaring fire. In the tale, January's images when he is fantasing about his would-be wife focus on food – the wedding feast is the most important element of the ceremony – and January then takes a number of rich wines as aphrodisiacs before he and his new wife retire to bed. His natural habitat is indoors; he loses control when the action moves to the garden.

May, conversely, is passive indoors and by night. After the marriage, however, she spends four days in bed (lines 673–80), and those four days are precisely astrologically described. The four days represent the four months between them, and the astrological phenomenon, the move of the moon from Saturn into Mercury, occurs mid way between January and May. January fatally takes May into the garden, and the adultery takes place, in the month of May (lines 920–21). In calendars, May is associated with hunting, hawking and gathering flowers, pursuits associated with **courtly love**. January's blindness renders him passive out of doors; this is the domain in which May is in control.

Damian is not as directly related to the astrological theme, but indirectly the association of fate with the scorpion (lines 845–47), suggests that January will be the victim of a sexual predator. The signs of the zodiac were each thought to govern a limb or organ of the body, and Scorpio ruled the male genitals.

Finally, the myth of Pluto's rape of Prosperpine is associated with the creation of the seasons. Astrological detail throughout the tale, and the suggestion that events may have been brought about by destiny, chance, nature or the stars (lines 755–57), all point towards an attempt to elevate an obscene fabliau by giving it a moralised universal meaning: the marriage of old age and youth is an unnatural conjunction.

BLINDNESS

Blindness is a common theme in literature because of its metaphorical potential, connecting the physical faculty of sight with moral and spiritual vision. As the Earl of Gloucester says in Shakespeare's *King Lear*, shortly after his eyes have been gouged out, 'I have no way, and therefore want no eyes;/ I stumbled when I saw' (*King Lear*, Act IV, scene 1, lines 19–20). The Merchant suggests that January has always been blind: blind to the risks of his choice of bride, blind to the sacramental nature of marriage, and, ultimately, physically blind. It is, however, possible for the reader to resist the opinions of the narrator and conclude that it is the Merchant who is truly blind. He cannot see the possibility of resurrecting any ideals in relationships between the sexes because he understands only materialism and lust. He is blind to the possibility of beauty, and that blindness infects every element of a tale which presents no redeeming features in character or action.

LANGUAGE AND STYLE

IMAGERY

Much of what goes to make *The Merchant's Tale* more than a simple fabliau derives from its imagery. Some of the fields of imagery are so extensive as to form separate thematic strands within the tale, such as the biblical images associated with Joseph and Mary, the calendar references which help to define the unnatural nature of January and May's relationship, and all the references to metaphorical and actual blindness which underpin the narrator's view of the hapless situation of the married man (see Themes).

    Underpinning the whole tale is a range of images referring to mercantile commodities, in particular to food and drink. These serve firstly to remind the reader of the true nature of the transaction January and May enter into, based on acquisitiveness and physical self-indulgence. They also, however, act as a reminder that the guiding intelligence behind the narrative is a merchant. It could be that Chaucer has the Merchant draw on these fields of imagery because they offer the comparisons which would come most readily to a man of his occupation, so lending plausibility to the narrator's character, or it could be that they indicate that the whole story is being transmitted from within a particular set of values according to which

Y

everything and everyone has their price. Food imagery is also closely connected with sex, and January is presented as an Epicurean – a follower of Epicurus, the ancient Roman scholar – devoting his life to the pursuit of physical pleasure.

May later turns the tables on January when she develops her craving for pears, and imagery associated with fruit plays a major part in the tale. The Tree of Knowledge in the Garden of Eden is conventionally seen as an apple tree; pears have a different and overtly sexual range of reference, which extends beyond the narrative source of the fabliau. The pear was related to human sexuality because of its physical resemblance to either the female breast or the male genitalia. Moreover, Chaucer, here and in *The Parson's Tale*, shows that he had knowledge of medieval scientific treatises and knew that the pear, or specifically the root of the pear tree, was valued for its contraceptive properties (see Carol Falvo Heffernan, 'Contraception and the Pear Tree Episode of Chaucer's *Merchant's Tale*', *Journal of English and Germanic Philology*, 94 (1995), 31–41). The suggestion could be that May is as eager to avoid conceiving with Damian as she is with January, that the latter's longed-for child will not be fathered by anyone, and that his failure to understand the true meaning of May's alleged craving for pears, as a craving for continuing sexual freedom, is yet another dimension of his blindness.

Early in the tale, January compares himself to a tree in full bloom before the fruit is fully formed, anticipating the tree in his garden in which the adultery will later take place. It is unsurprising that horticultural imagery is also threaded through this tale. Clearly there are references to the Garden of Eden from Genesis 2, but they are interwoven with allusions to the **allegorical** garden of **courtly love** in the long French medieval romance, *The Romance of the Rose*, and to the spiritual paradise described in Eustace Deschamps's *Miroir de Mariage* ('Mirror of Marriage') (see Themes on Anti-Feminism). The allegorical vision of heaven as a garden in the Old Testament book the Song of Solomon is obviously **parodied** and debased because January's garden is designed for sex (see Commentaries, lines 920–72). But of all the complex contributions to the garden imagery, the pagan garden of Parnassus is most easily overlooked. In the story of the Rape of Proserpine (see Commentaries on lines 1007–63), Pluto, like January, suffers from sexual desire in his old age and takes a wife in order to beget heirs and for bodily comfort. The details of Pluto and Proserpine's first night of marriage are similar to those in *The Merchant's Tale*. Although Pluto is King of the Underworld, his brother, Jupiter, arranges for Proserpine to spend every spring above ground. She does this in a specially constructed paradise garden, called Parnassus. So although Pluto and Proserpine here appear chiefly in their medieval guise as king and queen of fairies, there are allusions to the original classical myth from which they are drawn. Prosperpine was the pagan goddess protecting women in pregnancy and childbirth, so January's stroking of May's womb as they leave the garden adds further ambiguity to the range of interpretations of the tale's ending.

Imagery of a different and more straightforward order provides the thrust of the plot and one of the main sources of humour in the tale, as the ground is prepared for the theft of January's key. One of Chaucer's favourite comic techniques is to introduce an idea through a **simile** or **metaphor** early in a story, in anticipation of its actual appearance later. Here January sees his young wife as pliable wax (line 218), then Damian makes an impression on May (line 766), so that by the time that May takes the impression of the garden key and Damian forges the counterfeit, the reader is convinced of the sexual connotations of the image. Key and keyhole images are commonly associated with sex, but Chaucer here embellishes the image so that when the details of Damian's action are described in lines 940–43 their comic impact as an extended metaphor for the anticipated sexual act itself is beyond doubt.

Finally the image of the mirror appears only once in the tale, line 370, when the narrator comments that in his search for a bride it is as if January has set up a mirror in the marketplace. The image is worth remarking because of the popularity of mirror imagery in medieval art and literature, used in various ways. Most straightforwardly, a text can be a mirror because it reflects a field of knowledge or belief, but it can also distort or reverse, as in the expression 'mirror-image', and it can add a new dimension as it does in Jan van Eyck's famous painting of Giovanni Arnolfini and his Wife. Painted less than fifty years after *The Canterbury Tales* were written, a mirror behind the couple shows two people entering the room, one of them commonly believed to be the artist himself. The mirror image in *The Merchant's Tale* suggests that January is a voyeur, as indeed is the narrator and the reader of *The Merchant's Tale* in taking a salacious interest in the outcome of the tale. The mirror also suggests indirect and possibly distorted vision, so contributes to the theme of blindness which pervades the tale. It may also suggest, however, that the whole tale is a mirror which warns the reader about marriage, a covert allusion to Deschamps' anti-feminist treatise, mentioned above (see also Themes, on Anti-Feminism), with which the original audience of *The Canterbury Tales* may have been familiar. It is for the reader to decide whether this mirror, deliberately angled by the narrator, offers a true or distorted image.

SPEECH

In his comic narratives, Chaucer uses **direct speech** in order to impart a flavour of the character that is speaking by giving them a singular manner, often poking fun at a particular social type. For example, he frequently uses **proverbs**, which are homely **rhetoric** or **low style**, to make fun of pretentious but ignorant characters like January. January's philosophy, by which he argues that it is better to marry a young woman than an older one, is thus supported by the view that a pike is better than 'pikerel', and that tender young veal is preferable to old beef. The use of proverbs in this context exposes pomposity and limited imagination. The reader is also aware of underlying proverbial wisdom which is set up in opposition to January's. The narrator has already warned,

> A wif wol laste, and in thyn hous endure,
> Wel lenger than thee list, paraventure. (lines 105–06)

The sentiment, later supported by the warnings of Justinus who is the narrator's surrogate within the tale, is more commonly expressed proverbially as, 'Marry in haste; repent at leisure'.

Placebo's voice is constructed around a different type of filler, the **cliché** and empty tag, the equivalents of 'upon my soul'. These fillers are a stylistic device deliberately used to create the illusion of a particular kind of speaker whose speech is low on content. Placebo is a **satirical** portrait of the flatterer who listens attentively to what his superior says, then repeats it back in different words, embellished with expressions which make it sound more authoritative, all in the guise of seriously considered advice.

Where January does aspire to greater heights of rhetoric, such as his lyrical quotation from the *Song of Songs* when he is making love to May (see Commentary on lines 920–72), or his imitation of the bereaved mothers whose children have been murdered by Herod (see Commentary on lines 1142–1206), the inappropriate context undercuts their potential to achieve a more elevated style. The reading of these speeches is coloured by the manner in which the narrator's voice functions: whenever the Merchant rises to use artificially elevated exclamations, **rhetorical questions** and repetitions, as in the lines 845–56, the subject matter does not support the inflation of style, so the effect is comic. **Tonally** the tale is infected by the narrator's negative value system. Consequently no voice can achieve elevation without implied derision.

The specific relationship between the narrator and his characters and consequently the tale's tone, is conveyed not only by the content of speech and unspoken thought which is reported, but by the manner of that reporting. Almost all of the first five hundred lines of the tale are given over to argument; there is very little in the way of other action. Much of that argument is put into direct speech as we have seen, conveying a flavour of comic character. The rest is reported indirectly. Whereas **direct speech** gives the illusion that the reader is witnessing the actual words of the character, **indirect speech** or thought is mediated by the reporting narrator.

In *The Merchant's Tale*, Chaucer has constructed in the Merchant a narrator whose views on marriage are diametrically opposed to those of the **protagonist**. As neither the Merchant nor January are 'real' people, what the reader is actually witnessing is Chaucer's experiment in the construction of sustained **irony**, where everything the narrator reports as January's considered opinion is reported sceptically. The effect is achieved through the selection of detail and by implied significant omission, both of which systematically undermine the credibility of the reported argument. The passage between lines 365 and 424 particularly rewards study in this con-nection, as at times it appears to slip into **free indirect speech,** where the reporting narrator is in control but some of the phraseology echoes what the reader has come to recognise as January's manner. These techniques are akin to Jane Austen's narrative technique, whereby characters' judgements are consistently undermined by a sceptical controlling narrator to great ironic effect.

NARRATIVE TECHNIQUES

The specific and overriding narrative technique of *The Merchant's Tale* is irony. Irony is directed at January by the Merchant and at the Merchant by

Chaucer. The Merchant's ironies directed at January sometimes take the form of undisguised sneers, like 'Thus seyde this olde knight, that was so wis' (line 54). On other occasions the irony works by insinuation, particularly in the presentation of sacred material: for example the description of the wedding ceremony (lines 488–96), where choice of syntax and vocabulary conspire to make the account of what should be the climax of the wedding and expression of its core values as off-hand as possible. Indeed a substantial amount of the ironic undermining of January's dreams and aspirations is carried by the tone and context in which biblical and sacramental references are presented; it is not the biblical reference itself that is ironic, but its placing, often directly next to a reference to something overtly carnal or profane. Chaucer's ironic undermining of the Merchant derives from the same areas. The systematic contrasting of January and May's situation and values with biblical examples exposes the fact that the Merchant allows for the existence of no other kind of woman except the Virgin Mary or May. Nothing that January says or does in the tale is obscene or blasphemous; all the obscenity and blasphemy derives from the Merchant's gloss on the actions. Hence, as in the *General Prologue* portrait where he is outwardly worthy but secretly engaged in sharp practices. Chaucer exposes the Merchant in his tale as outwardly aloof and authoritative, while all the time he is pursuing a personal grudge and unhealthy fixation with his own distorted view of relations between the sexes. The impression may be of a complex character, but the Merchant is a product of the intricate layering of the tale's narrative technique. In this way Chaucer both creates a character but simultaneously offers an evaluation of the package of attitudes, values and beliefs which make up that character.

    Irony pervades the tone of the narrative, but other influences dictate its structure. The pear tree plot is a fabliau, and fabliau as a literary genre is characterised by fast-paced action; there is no need to develop characters which are simply functions of the plot and set up for derision, and no need to stop to explore philosophical issues, the inner thoughts or outward appearance of those involved. Romance, on the other hand, is a highly stylised form which indulges in long set-piece descriptio from landscape and weather to the appearance of the lovers and the afflictions they suffer when love is unrequited, the texts of speeches, songs and letters, exclamatory interventions from the narrator, and overtly embellished transitions from one part of the plot to the next. *The Merchant's Tale* is, in these terms, a stylistic hybrid. An audacious first third of the tale is given over to pondering the pros and cons of January's proposed marriage. Views are expressed by January, by Placebo and Justinus, and by the narrator himself. These views are more than amply supported by citation of learned authority. Once the plot gets underway, it moves sporadically at fabliau pace, but is held up from time to time by, for example, the description of Damian's love-sickness (562–82), which is followed by an astrological **digressio** (lines 583–89). Typically, a piece of fast-moving and down-to-earth narrative, such as the passage in which May makes her excuses to January, goes to the privy, reads the letter and disposes of it (lines 734–42), is juxtaposed with a rhetorically over-inflated intervention by the narrator (lines 755–64). The effect is to draw attention to both styles by their incongruity. As the balance gradually shifts from debate to action, which accelerates as the tale approaches its inevitable conclusion, the reader encounters the tale's major structural joke, for, falling back on the conventions of high romance, Chaucer abandons Damian up the tree, May and January in the garden, in order to indulge in a leisurely digression of exactly one hundred and one lines (lines 1007–1107) in fairyland. The effect is one of comic suspense, but the Pluto and Proserpine passage is also a literary joke which highlights Chaucer as artist-at-play, and demonstrates that although he may let the fictional Merchant control the tone of the tale, he alone controls its structure and pulls the strings.

Diction

The diction of *The Merchant's Tale* is crafted to present the reader with affronting oppositions, thereby supporting the broader **ironic** techniques of the narrative. Diction is perverted to suit **tone**. A number of high rhetorical devices are used in a way designed to undercut. For example, the **descriptio** of May is provided in the context of an old man lying in bed enjoying a sexual fantasy. Elsewhere, the contrast of Damian's love letter with the gratuitously explicit description of its fate in the privy, and the details of January's appearance in bed – which are the Merchant's observations, not May's – draw attention to vocabulary which is as far removed from the conventions of love-literature as it is possible to be.

Towards the end of the tale, the narrator, having amply demonstrated his easy command of Latinate vocabulary, of biblical language and of a wide range of classical learning, abruptly warns that he is a 'rude man', in the sense of 'plain' or 'unlearned', who 'kan nat glose', that is he is unable to use delicate **circumlocution** (lines 1139–40), then describes May and Damian's sexual embrace in a completely blunt manner. Shortly afterwards, when January's sight is restored, the narrator reports speech which uses very direct vocabulary to describe what January has just seen. Reading the tale as a fully developed drama, which it is not, one might say that the Merchant is determined to shock, and deliberately offend the pilgrims to jolt them out of any romantic illusions about marriage they may still harbour. January speaks as plainly as he does out of his own shock at catching his wife in the act of having sexual intercourse with his servant in a tree.

Another way of analysing what is going on is to consider that *The Merchant's Tale* is Chaucer's experiment in systematic *dis*illusion, which he characterises in the person of the Merchant, and that, as Alfred David has put it, he 'lifts the veil of poetry revealing obscenity' as surely as Damian lifts May's smock. The effect is complex: the tale cannot be described as wholly or simply comic and its joylessness, conveyed through a systematic devaluing and stripping away of poetic diction, may well lead the reader to re-evaluate the relationship between life and art.

PART FOUR

EXTENDED COMMENTARIES

TEXT 1 (LINES 99–149)

A wyf is Goddes yifte verraily;
Alle othere manere yiftes hardily,   100
As londes, rentes, pasture, or commune,
Or moebles, alle been yiftes of Fortune,
That passen as a shadwe upon a wal.
But drede nat, if pleynly speke I shal,
A wif wol laste, and in thyn hous endure,   105
Wel lenger than thee list, paraventure.
Mariage is a ful greet sacrement.
He which that hath no wyf, I holde him shent;
He liveth helplees and al desolat, –
I speke of folk in seculer estaat.   110
And herke why, I sey nat this for noght,
That womman is for mannes helpe ywroght.
The hie God, whan he hadde Adam maked,
And saugh him al allone, bely-naked;
God of his grete goodnesse seyde than,   115
'Lat us now make an helpe unto this man
Lyk to himself'; and thanne He made him Eve.
Heere may ye se, and heerby may ye preve,
That wyf is mannes helpe and his confort;
His paradis terrestre, and his disport.   120
So buxom and so vertuous is she,
They moste nedes live in unitee.
O flessh they been, and o fleesh, as I gesse,
Hath but oon herte, in wele and in distresse.
    A wyf, a, Seinte Marie, *benedicite*,   125
How mighte a man han any adversitee
That hath a wyf? Certes, I kan nat seye.
The blisse which that is bitwixe hem tweye
Ther may no tonge telle, or herte thinke.

If he be povre, she helpeth him to swinke;   130
She kepeth his good, and wasteth never a deel;
Al that hire housbonde lust, hire liketh weel;
She seith nat ones 'nay', whan he seith 'ye.'
'Do this,' seith he; 'Al redy sire,' seith she.
O blisful ordre of wedlok precious,   135
Thou art so murye, and eek so vertuous,
And so commended and appreved eek
That every man that halt him worth a leek,
Upon his bare knees oughte al his lyf
Thanken his God that him hath sent a wyf,   140
Or elles preye to God him for to sende
A wyf, to laste unto his lives ende.
For thanne his lyf is set in sikernesse;
He may nat be deceyved, as I gesse,
So that he werke after his wyves reed.   145
Thanne may he boldely beren up his heed,
They been so trewe, and therwithal so wise;
For which, if thou wolt werken as the wise,
Do alwey so as wommen wol thee rede.

This passage is generally understood to be spoken in the voice of the
Merchant narrator. It follows his reference to Theophrastus, the learned
authority on why it is not good to take a wife, and is set up as a mock
refutation of that argument. Consequently it contains a number of
rhetorical devices designed to give weight and emphasis to the argument,
all of which are overplayed for comic and **ironic** effect. It addresses its
audience directly in the **second person** and casts that audience as male.
The reader can imagine the implied dramatic context whereby the narrator
is addressing the predominantly male audience of fellow-pilgrims, and read
as a fellow man, or can resist the assumptions of the narrator and read
sceptically, from a woman's point of view.

   Both of the first two lines end in an adverb, lending them emphasis.
It also means that there is a rhythm change as it gives both lines **feminine
endings**. The first line states that a wife is the gift of God. The following
lines 100–103 contrast a wife with the gifts of Fortune. Fortune is a
common medieval **personification**, ironically in this context represented as

a fickle woman who gives and takes away on a turn of her wheel. The Merchant's inventory of the other gifts exposes his personal value system, for they are all material goods; consequently and by implication he equates a wife with material possessions. The **simile** of the shadow on the wall refers to the passage of time and the inevitable loss of sunshine, fitting well with the other references to the passage of time and season in the tale that follows. 'Verraily' (line 99) and 'hardily' (line 100) are then followed by the third adverb in this verse paragraph, 'pleynly' (line 104), signalling a **tonal** shift as the Merchant finishes with the warning that a wife, being more durable than the other gifts of fortune, may last longer than you want. Emphasis is given to the idea of the wife's tenacity by stating it twice, the second time reminding the audience that she will be in the husband's house. The final 'paraventure' (line 106), means 'by chance', so reverts to the idea of fortune, implicitly reminding the audience that fortune can be bad as well as good. The plain talking of the Merchant is something which the reader will encounter more than once in the tale: on each of its occurrences it signals the prurience of a closed mind which elsewhere shows itself to be a mind capable of delicacy, but chooses not to be on the subject of sexual relations.

The second verse paragraph also opens with a one-line assertive statement in the form of a declarative sentence. In it, the narrator states that marriage is a great sacrament of the Church, but he does not go on to elaborate. A sacrament is a ritual of the Church in which something mystical is believed to occur in the form of the spiritual intervention of God to sanctify a transformation in the participants. In the Middle Ages, the sequence of seven sacraments was frequently illustrated in Church art and was familiar to the laity as an important part of their spiritual armament against the devil and his works. The seven sacraments are Baptism, Confirmation, Marriage, Eucharist, Penance, Ordination and Extreme Unction. Marriage as a sacrament was said to have derived its sanctity from God's creation of Eve for Adam, which is what the narrator goes on to relate. He also points out that unlike the other sacraments, marriage is available only to those who are secular, that is, not in religious orders, implying what the Church actually preached, that the married condition was less holy than clerical celibacy notwithstanding its sacramental status. A secular man without a wife is 'helpless'; a wife is man's help – the word occurs three times – as Eve was for Adam. Far from elaborating on the sanctity of the married state, the **irony** of the passage develops, as the reader is led to consider the story of Adam and Eve and how Eve was a legendary hindrance rather than a help to her husband, working against rather than for his best interests. Adam's own responsibility for the Fall is not considered here; instead Adam is described as 'bely-naked' (line 114), an expression which first suggests his innocence and vulnerability. As the passage progresses, however, the narrator's imagined Garden of Eden, with its famously naked and unashamed inhabitants, takes on more carnal connotations, as Eve is described as Adam's recreation and earthly paradise. He dwells, too, on that element of the marriage ceremony in which the man and woman are said to become one flesh. Whether Adam and Eve's relationship was physical while they were still in paradise was a topic of theological debate in the Middle Ages. St Augustine was of the view that the first man and woman did have a sexual relationship, but it was of a kind that no human being living after the Fall could understand or imagine, and therefore it was sinful to think about it. It is clear that this narrator has no such inhibitions and believes that Adam was having a delightful sexually active life in paradise until Eve went and ruined it for him. Rhetorical flourishes, such as the aside in line 111, give the illusion that the reader is overhearing a particular speaking voice addressing an audience.

There are more rhetorical flourishes in the third verse paragraph, which opens with a **rhetorical question** containing two expletives, one of them in Latin. This passage enters into a mock flight of imaginative fantasy as the narrator creates the behaviour and voice of an 'ideal' wife. The passage is full of repetitions and **hyperbole**, deliberately overinflating the picture of the wife to ridiculous lengths for comic effect. The assertion that marriage is so blissful that no one can describe it, ironically suggests that this bliss may be indescribable because it is non-existent. Further high-style **tropes** follow as the narrator goes on to address marriage itself in a brief eulogy. Again irony is the main effect, as the overinflated style contrasts with, for example, the low-style idiomatic reference to leeks. The image of the man praying on his bare knees is again comic, as, although the prayer he is supposed to be offering up is one of thanks, the posture is reminiscent of penance. Consequently line 144, in which the narrator states that no man will be deceived, is heavily ironic, followed by the suggestion that he will be able to hold up his head in public provided he does everything his wife tells him to. The final ironic point is emphasised by the rhyming of 'wise' with itself in lines 147 and 148, bracketed closely between two lines, 145 and 149, which end in 'reed'/'rede' meaning advice. The implication is that a wife's advice is not worth having, and, perhaps, the 'advice' that the narrator has just been so enthusiastically giving is not reliable either.

TEXT 2   (LINES 583–653)

Parfourned hath the sonne his ark diurne;
No lenger may the body of him sojurne
On th'orisonte, as in that latitude.   585
Night with his mantel, that is derk and rude,
Gan oversprede the hemisperie aboute;
For which departed is this lusty route
Fro Januarie, with thank on every side.
Hoom to hir houses lustily they ride,   590
Where as they doon hir thinges as hem leste,
And whan they sye hir time, goon to reste.
Soone after that, this hastif Januarie
Wolde go to bedde, he wolde no lenger tarye,
He drinketh ypocras, clarree and vernage   595
Of spices hoote, t'encreesen his corage;
And many a letuarie hath he ful fyn,
Swiche as the cursed monk, daun Constantin,
Hath writen in his book *De Coitu;*
To eten hem alle he nas no thing eschu.   600
And to his privee freendes thus seyde he:
'For Goddes love, as soone as it may be,
Lat voiden al this hous in curteys wise.'
And they han doon right as he wol devise.
Men drinken, and the travers drawe anon.   605
The bride was broght abedde as stille as stoon;
And whan the bed was with the preest yblessed,
Out of the chambre hath every wight him dressed;
And Januarie hath faste in armes take
His fresshe May, his paradis, his make.   610
He lulleth hire, he kisseth hire ful ofte;

With thikke brustles of his berd unsofte,
Lyk to the skin of houndfissh, sharp as brere –
For he was shave al newe in his manere –
He rubbeth hire aboute hir tendre face,   615
And seyde thus, 'Allas, I moot trespace
To yow, my spouse, and yow greetly offende,
Er time come that I wil doun descende.
But nathelees, considereth this,' quod he,
'Ther nis no werkman, whatsoevere he be,   620
That may bothe werke wel and hastily;
This wol be doon at leyser parfitly.
It is no fors how longe that we pleye;
In trewe wedlok coupled be we tweye;
And blessed be the yok that we been inne,   625
For in oure actes we mowe do no sinne.
A man may do no sinne with his wyf,
Ne hurte himselven with his owene knyf;
For we han leve to pleye us by the lawe.'
Thus laboureth he til that the day gan dawe;   630
And thanne he taketh a sop in fyn clarree,
And upright in his bed thanne sitteth he,
And after that he sang ful loude and cleere,
And kiste his wif, and made wantown cheere.
He was al coltissh, ful of ragerye,   613
And ful of jargon as a flekked pye.
The slakke skin aboute his nekke shaketh.
Whil that he sang, so chaunteth he and craketh.
But God woot what that May thoughte in hir herte,
Whan she him saugh up sittinge in his sherte,   640
In his night-cappe, and with his nekke lene;
She preyseth nat his pleying worth a bene.
Thanne seide he thus, 'My reste wol I take;
Now day is come, I may no lenger wake.'
And doun he leyde his heed, and sleep til prime.   645
And afterward, whan that he saugh his time,
Up riseth Januarie; but fresshe May
Heeld hire chambre unto the fourthe day,

As usage is of wives for the beste.

For every labour somtime moot han reste,   650

Or elles longe may he nat endure;

This is to seyn, no lives creature,

Be it of fissh, or brid, or beest, or man.

The type of **circumlocution** used to mark and embellish a transition in the plot in high **romance** is here parodied as the narrator takes seven lines to impart the information 'night fell'. Rhetorically, he has proceeded from the **apostrophe** of the preceding paragraph to **descriptio.** The comic effect is achieved not only because the **tone** of these rhetorical digressions is too elevated for the context, but because January is in such a hurry to get May into bed, and the leisurely pace of the narrative seems to be conspiring against him. For the planetary detail, all quite redundant to the plot, Chaucer draws on his own genuine interest in astronomy, which he wrote about elsewhere in his prose treatise on *The Astrolabe*, an instrument used for measuring the movements of heavenly bodies. He draws on this type of material in his high-style romances, notably *Troilus and Criseyde* and *The Knight's Tale*, but here stylistic devices commonly used to create a sense of a rarefied world of finer sentiment cast into relief the moral poverty and 'graphic ugliness' (Muscatine, 1957, 234) of the action. The suspension of the action is further drawn out by another three lines which tell us that the wedding guests rode home 'lustily' and did whatever it was they wanted to before going to bed, all completely meaningless and unnecessary detail.

January, unlike the narrator, is of course 'hastif' (line 593) (hasty) to go to bed, and the pace of the narrative quickens with the list of aphrodisiacs he takes. The information that on his marriage night he needs sex aids and a manual, reminds the reader that he is old and, therefore, possibly impotent, and also enhances the sense that this marriage is in all respects unnatural and empty of genuine feeling. As the narrative moves in closer on the scene from the giddying stylistic and geographical height of the heavens, January speaks. His speech opens with a blasphemous invocation of God's love, reminding the reader that there is little of either God or love in these circumstances, despite the conventional veneer given them by the marriage sacrament, and the information, six lines later, that the priest blessed the marriage bed. The privacy he desires is, however, created by the drawing of the bed curtains, a detailed action preparing for the first occasion May will have sex with January, in marked contrast to the lifting of the smock in her later encounter with Damian.

If January's lechery is unseemly and even disgusting as described by the narrator, May's frigidity on her wedding night is chilling. The description of the bride as stony, however much the reader may be repelled by January, contributes to the unremitting negativity of the passage. What follows is a description of a wedding night which could not be further from the romantic ideal. January, true to his calendar model (see Themes, on Calendars and Astrology), is active all night, and, so far as the reader can tell, May is completely passive. May's name here, and at numerous other points in the tale, is preceded by the adjective 'fressh' (line 610), initially suggesting quite neutrally her youth, beauty and innocence, but gradually becoming more **ironically** associated with the sense of sexual precocity. Here, too, May is January's paradise, recalling the earlier references to Adam and Eve, but also anticipating the paradise garden in which January will be betrayed.

The details of January's love-making move the narrative down from high romance to a level of gratuitously ugly naturalistic detail. Earlier, January compared himself to the predatory pike fish (line 208); now the narrator uses an unflattering **simile** comparing the stubble on January's chin with the bristles on a dogfish, to add arresting imaginative detail to the first of the tale's grotesque love scenes. There is similar graphic detail offered later in the passage when January sits up in bed in the morning and the reader is treated to the information that he was wearing a nightcap, that he sang loudly and behaved in a skittish manner so that the slack skin round his neck wobbled. In his comic writing, Chaucer frequently draws portraits of people who have odd physical characteristics, such as the wart on the Miller's nose, the Reeve's long thin legs, Absolon's strange hair-style in *The Miller's Tale*, the Friar's extreme portliness, but rarely is the reader's response more likely to be one of disgust rather than amusement as is the case here. January's pillow talk is no more romantic, as he describes what he is about to do as 'trespace' (line 616), that is to cause offence. For him it is 'pleye' (line 623) which he can, as a lawfully married man, take at his 'leyses' (line 622). January asserts that whatever he does to his wife cannot be accounted sin because of the sanctity of marriage, just as a man cannot hurt himself with his own knife. The foolishness of the second statement by implication undermines the first: both are nonsense and, indeed, the medieval Church preached clearly that a lack of sexual continence and moderation in marriage was as sinful as fornication. Whatever the view of the Church, however, it is true that the law offered little protection to a woman whose husband abused her, as she was his property.

There is some indication of what will come later when the focus finally returns to May. The narrator finds her feelings inaccessible and is unable to tell how she felt, yet the reader is informed that she thought January's 'playing' to be worthless. This statement suggests a certain sexual connoisseurship on May's part, not entirely in keeping with her presumed status as a young, innocent bride. The reader may remember that she was earlier described as a young woman of the town (line 411).

As the passage ends, the narrative draws back from the specific detail of the scene to its more emblematic significance, as January becomes passive by day, and May stays in her room for four days. Both details have significance in relation to the tale's other levels of meaning (see Themes, on Calendars and Astrology). Finally the narrator declares that all creation observes the rule that rest must follow labour. This is also blasphemous by implication as it invokes in a purely sexual context the idea of the Sabbath, the symbolic seventh day on which God, having created the world, rested and which all creation should emulate.

TEXT 3   (LINES 1108–41)

Now lat us turne again to Januarie,
That in the gardyn with his faire May
Singeth ful murier than the papejay,   1110
'Yow love I best, and shal, and oother noon.'
So longe aboute the aleyes is he goon,
Til he was come againes thilke pyrie
Where as this Damyan sitteth ful myrie
An heigh among the fresshe leves grene.   1115
    This fresshe May, that is so bright and sheene,
Gan for to sike, and seyde, 'Allas, my side.
Now sire,' quod she, 'for aught that may bitide,
I moste han of the peres that I see,
Or I moot die, so soore longeth me   1120
To eten of the smale peres grene.

Help, for hir love that is of hevene queene.
I telle yow wel, a womman in my plit
May han to fruit so greet an appetit
That she may dien, but she of it have.'   1125
    'Allas,' quod he, 'that I ne had heer a knave
That koude climbe. Allas, allas,' quod he,
'For I am blind.' 'Ye, sire, no fors,' quod she;
'But wolde ye vouche sauf, for Goddes sake,
The pyrie inwith youre armes for to take,   1130
For wel I woot that ye mistruste me,
Thanne sholde I climbe wel ynogh,' quod she,
'So I my foot mighte sette upon youre bak.'
    'Certes,' quod he, ' theron shal be no lak,
Mighte I yow helpen with myn herte blood.'   1135
He stoupeth down, and on his bak she stood,
And caughte hire by a twiste, and up she gooth.
Ladies, I prey yow that ye be nat wrooth;
I kan nat glose, I am a rude man –
And sodeynly anon this Damyan   1140
Gan pullen up the smok, and in he throng.

The passage resumes the narrative of January and May's fateful visit to the
garden, following a hundred-line digression in which Pluto and Proserpine
debate the rights and wrongs of what May is about to do. The opening is
typical of **romance** in which the transitions between parallel actions are
formally pointed out. The technique of handling multiple scenes of action
in French romance is called *entrelacement*, literally 'interlacing'. Just as
Chaucer held up January's progress into bed with May by **parodying** the
leisurely and embellished style of high romance (see Text 2), here, too, he
plays with the reader by elegantly drawing out the progress of May's
encounter with Damian in the garden towards its inelegant conclusion.

    The passage continues with brief **allusions** to the world of love
poetry. January sings happily like a parrot. The association of parrots with
tame, or pet, lovers derives from the erotic poetry of Ovid, well known to
the Middle Ages, whose lady Corinna has a pet parrot. Then, when the
lovers are described as walking amongst the winding paths in the garden
before they reach the pear tree, Chaucer is echoing the great medieval

allegorical love poem, *The Romance of the Rose*, in which the lover has to wind his way through a maze of paths in his garden in search of his perfect rose. But the conclusion here is rather different. Damian sits waiting in the pear tree like the serpent in the garden of Eden, reminding the reader that this is a tale as much of archetypal betrayal as of love.

May, as is customary, is described as 'fresshe' (line 1116) (see Text 2), before she begins to speak. Again, Chaucer parodies the conventions of **courtly love** as May gives voice to a mortal longing. By this point in the tale, 'fresshe' **connotes** sexual readiness rather than innocence, and May's longing for pears, with all their sexual symbolism (see Language and Style, on Imagery) ironically conceals an evident longing to have sex with Damian. May's invocation of the Virgin Mary, Queen of Heaven, at this point is particularly inappropriate, but reminds the reader of the comparisons and contrasts between the superficially similar Joseph and Mary and January and May, which has been threaded throughout the tale. May speaks with delightful ambiguity of women in her 'plit' (line 1123) (plight). All the connotations are sexual; the ambiguity lies in the potential different understandings of where May is at this moment in the cycle of desire of conception, pregnancy and birth. Her great appetite for fruit, in the light of popular comparisons of the pear with male genitalia, needs no further explanation. A contemporary anonymous erotic lyric, in which the ancient horticultural procedure of grafting different types of fruit on to the same tree, is used as the focus of an obscene joke, and provides a context for the various available layers of innuendo in May's little speech:

> I have a new garden
> And new is begun
> Such another garden
> Know I not under sun.
>
> In the midst of my garden
> Is a pear tree set
> And it will no pear bear
> But a Pear Janet.
>
> The fairest maid of this town
> Prayed me

For to graft her a graft
Of my pear tree.

When I had grafted them
All at her will,
The wine and the ale
She did in fill.

And I grafted her
Right up in her home:
And by that day twenty weeks
It was quick in her womb.

That day twelve months
That maid I met:
She said it was a Pear Robert
But no Pear Janet.

[R.T. Davies, ed., *Medieval English Lyrics*, London: Faber and Faber,
1966, 69, p.158, reproduced here with modernised spellings].

Blind January's regret that he does not have a knave who can climb to satisfy his wife's longing, is heavily **ironic**, given that Damian is already in the tree. May's solution, that he should embrace the tree so that she can put her foot on his back, puts him both physically and **metaphorically** under her foot. Also, given the development of a plethora of sexual images, it is frequently suggested that January's embracing the tree connotes a grotesque masturbation as May leaves him for her preferred sexual partner.

The final paragraph swiftly narrates the ensuing action, as May climbs into the tree and sexual union with the waiting Damian. The apparent sudden shock of the single line describing that union is rhetorical rather than actual, achieved by the plain diction and two verbs, 'gan pullen' and 'throng' (line 1141) in quick succession. In fact, the action has been prepared for by elaborate metaphorical foreplay, which began with May's suggestive signs to Damian (line 438) and reach their climax in January's embrace of the tree trunk. The lifting of the smock contrasts shockingly with the modest drawing of the bed curtains which preceded May's union with January on their wedding night (see Text 1).

The narrator's claim that he cannot gloss over the action is deeply cynical and draws immediate attention back to the character of the Merchant. Firstly, the claim is patently untrue, as this narrator has just demonstrated his ability not only to handle erudite reference, but romance diction with all its **elliptical** flexibility, so the brutally direct line 1141 is unpoetic for effect. The paragraph not only places the person of the narrator in the foreground, but the dramatic situation of the narrative. The Merchant has hitherto been addressing himself to an audience of men, courting their sympathy on the subject of marriage; here he addresses ladies. The only ladies on the pilgrimage to Canterbury are a handful of nuns, to whom the whole tale, never mind its climax, would be shocking, and the Wife of Bath, conversely unlikely to be shocked by anything at all. Here as elsewhere (see Commentaries, lines 443–76) Chaucer may choose to make his layers of narrative permeable, so that the playful apology is as much addressed to the ladies of the court, who are the envisaged audience of *The Canterbury Tales*, as it is to the fictional ladies on their way to Canterbury.

PART FIVE

BACKGROUND

GEOFFREY CHAUCER'S LIFE AND WORK

Geoffrey Chaucer was born in London in the early 1340s, most probably in 1343, the son, possibly the only son, of John Chaucer and his wife Agnes. The family originated in Ipswich where they had been called 'de Dynyngton' or 'le Taverner' and it seems likely that Geoffrey Chaucer's great-grandfather had been a tavern keeper. Geoffrey's grandfather, Robert de Dynyngton, appears to have worked for a merchant, but when the merchant died in a brawl in 1302 Robert inherited some of his property. The family were now far more prosperous and as a result of this change in fortune they also changed their name. They took the name of their dead benefactor: Chaucer.

They settled in London where John Chaucer, Geoffrey's father, became a very prosperous wine merchant. He supplied wine to the king's cellars, supervising imports from France. He was influential and successful and was heavily involved in the business and political affairs of the city. His wealth and connections meant that he could provide his young son with many advantages, beginning with Geoffrey's enrolment as a page in the royal household.

A page was a boy between the ages of ten and seventeen who was an attendant in the house of a noble family. Effectively he was a servant but in this way a boy would learn about polite society and hopefully be accepted by a patron, someone who would take an interest in him and help his career. The young Geoffrey became a page to the Countess of Ulster, the king's daughter-in-law, and eventually served her husband, Prince Lionel.

It was in the service of Prince Lionel that Geoffrey was captured in France. Edward III made an unsuccessful attempt to gain the French throne in 1359 and Geoffrey Chaucer is named among those for whom a ransom was paid. After this, he seems to have entered the direct service of the king, though his diplomatic skills appear to have been more in demand than his military expertise. He was sent on diplomatic missions to Spain, France and Italy over the next few years and some of his business seems to have been of a very secret nature.

Chaucer's social standing was also improved by his marriage in 1365 to Philippa Payne (or de Roet), a lady in the household of Queen Philippa, Edward III's wife. Philippa's sister Katherine was the mistress, and eventually the third wife, of John of Gaunt, the rich and powerful son of Edward III. Chaucer's marriage to Philippa therefore connected him more intimately to the circle of John of Gaunt and the royal court. John's son by his first marriage would later become King Henry IV and Chaucer's nephews were therefore half-brothers to the future king.

Chaucer's daily life does not seem to have been drastically affected by his family connections. In fact, in 1374 he was appointed to a new position with the customs department in London, a move which took him away from court. He was responsible for checking the quantities of wool, sheepskins and hides being shipped abroad so that the correct export duty could be charged. He was still sent overseas on state business and these trips probably brought him into contact with the works of the great European poets.

In 1389 he was appointed to a new position: Clerk of the King's Works. Still a civil servant, his new post meant that he was in charge of overseeing the building and repair of the king's properties. He supervised the workmen, paid the wages and saw that the plans were properly implemented. However, paying the wages proved to be more of a problem than it sounds. Chaucer was robbed, certainly once but possibly three times in the space of four days, as he attempted to deliver the money. It may have been a relief, therefore, when he was instructed to give up the post a few months later.

Chaucer now retired from the king's service but he continued to receive annual payments from the court, together with gifts such as a fur-trimmed, scarlet gown from the future Henry IV and an annual tun (252 gallons) of wine from Richard II. An occasional poem on the state of his purse ensured that his pension arrived on time but most of his creative energy was focused on one work, *The Canterbury Tales*. This was the last decade of Chaucer's life. He died on 25 October 1400, *The Canterbury Tales* still unfinished. He was buried in one of the more humble chapels in Westminster Abbey but his body was later moved to the east aisle of the south transept, where he became the first tenant of 'Poets' Corner'.

Chaucer and italy

The Merchant's Tale is set in Italy. In part this is a device to distance the reader from the characters in the tale, and **romances** commonly had exotic settings. Chaucer's other **fabliaux**, however, are set closer to home; the tales told by the Miller and Reeve are set in Oxford and East Anglia respectively. The Italian setting, therefore, is another marker of the mixed pedigree of *The Merchant's Tale*. Chaucer was also familiar with the real Italy, having travelled there as part of royal commissions in 1372 and 1378, and could well have met the great Italian poets of his time, Giovanni Boccaccio, author of another famous medieval book of framed tales, *The Decameron*, and the great poet of love, Francesc Petrarch. The reason for Chaucer's inclusion on these commissions was because of his fluency in the Italian language, which he had learnt through his father's trading relationships with Genoese merchants. On his second journey he visited the seat of the great, if legendarily corrupt, Visconti, dukes of Milan. The Visconti were owners of an extensive library where Chaucer may have extended his reading of Italian vernacular literature. Certainly *The Clerk's Tale*, which immediately precedes that of the Merchant and is also set in Lombardy, derives from versions of the story by both Boccaccio and Petrarch. Fabliau, too, as a genre was more popular in Italian and French literature than in English, and the pear tree story exists in one version in an Italian tale.

Chaucer and trade

Chaucer's father was a prosperous wine merchant from Ipswich who secured his son a position as pageboy at the royal court from which Geoffrey built a career as royal servant. The audience for whom Chaucer wrote *The Canterbury Tales* was aristocratic and London-based, but he himself had mercantile origins. The period through which Chaucer lived was one in which merchants thrived and grew in status. Cities had begun to increase in size as the Black Death had left many men from the country without masters. They had come to towns and cities to find an independent living. English society for those who survived the plague was affluent and offered a larger market for consumer goods than before. As the demands of the nobility and their estates were joined by the crafts and tradesmen of the cities, any moderately substantial town came to represent a market for essential and luxury goods as substantial as that of the average landed estate. England imported all manner of goods. The main traffic was across the North Sea from the Low Countries, but the major ports on the other side, like Antwerp and Bruges, offered direct access to Danzig (modern Gdanske), the Black Sea, and points east. As far as exports were concerned, English wool was still in demand in all the cloth-producing centres of the Low Countries, but England was also poised on the brink of becoming a major cloth-producer and exporter too.

The occupation and way of life of the merchant differed substantially from that of the nobility or the peasant; he neither tilled the soil nor provided military service, and taxes, to the crown. He also suffered from the teachings of the Church that to store up treasures in this world inevitably meant to suffer in the next. But busy men of affairs could not afford to devote their lives to penance and prayer, and inevitably reaped the material rewards in terms of creature comforts for their hard work. The urban merchant class, therefore, became major benefactors of charitable causes. In the Gospel of Matthew, Chapter 25, Christ preaches that at Doomsday the sheep would be separated from the goats according to six precepts, which came to be known as the Corporal Works of Mercy: feeding the hungry, giving drink to the thirsty, clothing the naked, visiting the sick, visiting prisoners and taking in travellers. These precepts became the merchants' salvation as they founded guilds and hospitals in the cities in which they lived for the purpose of engaging in charitable acts of conspicuous expenditure, and used these precepts when making their wills in order to off-load their material gains and secure a passage to heaven.

Anxious about their spiritual destiny, for it is as difficult for a rich man to enter the kingdom of heaven as it is for a camel to pass through the eye of a needle (Matthew 19, 24), the members of the burgeoning and largely unrecognised merchant class were equally anxious to acquire social recognition. Many medieval merchants married the daughters of, or married their daughters to, the sons of impoverished members of the gentry. By this means they not only gained access to closed social and court circles, but also found ways to become MPs and members of royal commissions and established for themselves an influence-base. More crucially, investment in land protected merchant capital against the vagaries of the market and offered security which reinvestment in shipping did not. Without the security of land, or indeed of city property, merchants ran great financial risks. Depreciation was low, and co-ownership of cargoes and ships spread the risks further, so that investments might be recovered within a year, but the merchant who did not have a source of rental income to supplement the profits of trade could easily fall into temporary debt. The demand for financial backers exceeded the supply, and capital investment was hard to secure, so merchants did have recourse to credit despite the Church's teaching about the sins of usury.

For its part, the landed marriage market was open to injections of mercantile cash because protracted war with France – the 'Hundred Years' War' – had been financed by heavy taxation. Land was easy to tax, but with no modern tax returns or effective means of getting the cash-rich man to declare how much he had, movable goods were less so. The period was one which saw the monarch currying favour with the City of London, the City governors being drawn from the wealthiest members of the urban merchant class, in order to gain access to mercantile wealth. The anonymous satirical debate, *Winner and Waster*, written in the 1370s, characterises Waster as a courtier-aristocrat prepared to share his wealth, and Winner, as a prudent merchant, whose wealth is less easy to access for the public purse. The main source of taxation of trade lay in the imposition of duties upon goods entering and leaving port, and customs accounts at all England's major ports were assiduously kept and returned to the Exchequer. Chaucer spent some part of his adult life as a controller of customs at the Port of London.

CHAUCER'S OTHER WORKS

Chaucer's work spans most of the major **genres** of medieval literature. The earliest works to survive are short ballads of love, although he is chiefly remembered as a narrative poet. Medieval authors tended to draw creatively on existing material which they saw as authoritative, rather than inventing new stories, so much of what Chaucer wrote he would have described as 'translation' – literally 'carrying across'. Sometimes his translations are indeed loosely translated reproductions of great works of European literature in English. This is the case with his earliest long work, the *Romaunt of the Rose*, a rendering of a long **allegorical** French poem about love, and his later *Boece*, a prose translation of *The Consolation of Philosophy*, an influential Latin work by the early Christian philosopher Boethius.

Elsewhere, however, Chaucer drew on old stories from the European tradition, creatively adapting them in his own ways to make them fit different narrative contexts and voices, and to convey new meanings. He wrote three 'dream visions', narratives in which the narrator tells of a dream he had which has cast particular light on a subject. The first of these, *The Book of the Duchess*, offered John of Gaunt oblique consolation on the death of his first wife, Blanche. *The Parlement of Fowles*, in which the dreamer sees a variety of species of birds debating the nature of romantic love, was probably written for a Valentine's Day event at court. The unfinished *House of Fame* has the dreamer 'Geffrey' carried into the heavens by an eagle to find out what is the appropriate material for poetry. In *The Legend of Good Women* the poet dreams that the God of Love rebukes him for telling stories of unfaithful women, and this encounter is followed by a collection of narrative accounts of the lives of female saints and martyrs. As a series of tales set within a unifying framework it offers a model which he was to re-use more adventurously in *The Canterbury Tales*.

A number of other unfinished poems and fragments of Chaucer's writing have survived, as well as his scientific prose *Treatise on the Astrolabe*. Chaucer's longest single narrative poem, however, is the great tragic love story of *Troilus and Criseyde*, set in antiquity during the war between Troy and Greece, which tells the story of Troilus, son of King Priam of Troy, who fell in love with the beautiful Criseyde, daughter of the disgraced Calchas who had betrayed the city. Troilus, with the help of Criseyde's uncle Pandarus woos and wins Criseyde, only to be deserted when she is sent over to the Greeks in exchange for a Trojan prisoner and seeks refuge in the arms of the Greek warrior Diomede. The poem incorporates philosophical commentary, high drama, and some of the most beautiful lyrical love poetry of its age.

THE CANTERBURY TALES

Chaucer died before he could finish *The Canterbury Tales*, but he did write an ending for the whole book in which he dedicated his life and writings to God. Here he commended his philosophical and religious writing, but retracted what modern readers consider his best work, his narrative fictions, the dream visions, *Troilus and Criseyde*, and those of *The Canterbury Tales* that 'incline to sin'. *The Canterbury Tales* was his hugely ambitious last project.

In the framing narrative a number of pilgrims meet in the Tabard Inn in Southwark to undertake a pilgrimage to the shrine of St Thomas à Becket in Canterbury Cathedral. Pilgrimages to the shrines of saints were a popular contemporary way of repenting for sins committed and for making peace with God in what was a pervasively Christian age. Many involved great danger and hardship, and English men and women set off on journeys, from which they often did not return, to the shrine of St James at Compostella in northern Spain, to Jerusalem and to Rome. The journey to Canterbury was not, however, a hard one, especially in springtime, so the possibility for a satirical treatment of the pilgrims is present in Chaucer's account from the beginning. The motives of many for undertaking this supposedly penitential journey to England's most popular shrine are unclear; for many it seems to have been a holiday outing.

The pilgrims represent a wide cross-section of Chaucer's contemporary society, but not one which is complete or ordered in any way, either socially or morally; rather the reader finds a variety of medieval people defined by their way of life or occupation. The game they become involved in is a storytelling competition whereby each pilgrim has to tell two stories on the way to Canterbury, two on the way back.

The scheme was never completed and scholars continue to argue about the intended order of the tales. None survives in Chaucer's own hand, and the manuscripts in which they were collected after his death arrange them differently. *The General Prologue* is there as a map, however, and the Parson's prose sermon appears before the author's epilogue. In the middle there are a number of fragments containing stories of knights and ladies in love, of tragedy, religion, and many riotously funny and sometimes obscene, narrative jokes. Some of the tales stand alone, but many are grouped or paired. It used to be thought that *The Merchant's Tale*, with the tales of the Wife of Bath, Clerk and Franklin, constituted a 'marriage group' within the whole. The only secular woman on the pilgrimage, the Wife of Bath, sets up an outrageous model of how women can and do manipulate marriage to their own ends. She is countered by the Clerk with his story of patient Griselda. The Merchant then tells his story of marital strife from the male point of view, before the Franklin defuses the whole debate with his tale of mutual give-and-take. There is something fruitful to be gained from this way of reading, provided one remembers that the order of the tales and even their allocation to tellers may be provisional, and that each of these tales has far more to offer the reader than a contribution to a debate on marriage alone.

HISTORICAL BACKGROUND

Many people in Chaucer's time saw signs of the expected end of the world. England was engaged in chronic warfare with France in what later became known as the Hundred Years War. Turbulence in Europe had led to schism in the Roman Catholic Church, the one recognised Church, so that for a while from 1378 there were two popes, one based in the Vatican, the other in Avignon in southern France. The middle of the fourteenth century had seen violent changes in the weather, with storms causing structural damage and years of ruined harvests. But above all, the outbreak of the plague, later known as the Black Death, had wiped out around one third of the population of Europe during the 1340s. No wonder people believed that God might be angry.

The Black Death not only caused psychological shock to all in society, but hastened social change. The structure of government and the economy in England had been based upon land ownership since the Norman Conquest of 1066, with nobility and country gentry holding land from the king according to their place in the hierarchy. In return for land ownership the king demanded military service as well as taxes to support the nation in peace and at war. The Church had a very similar structure. Archbishops and bishops were its great lords who acted as ministers, diplomats and advisers to the monarch. The church, too, supported itself by land ownership by diocese, monastery or parish, each with its tenants. Those who prayed and those who fought made up the first two of the three 'estates', which was how contemporary theorists saw society. Those who worked, that is everyone else, made up the third estate.

The third estate had long ceased to be made up of peasants, however, but also included fabulously wealthy international merchants and well-to-do urban craftsmen. The Black Death accelerated the growth of a varied urban life with its own complex social structures, and of a monetary economy where wealth could be measured not by land but by cash. The death of so many of the population assisted the collapse of old structures by creating a labour shortage and, consequently, greater social and geographical mobility. Many of Chaucer's pilgrims represent 'new money', only the Knight and the Squire representing the old ruling class. The Merchant is part of the new urban patriciate whose wealth is tied up in movable goods and cash rather than land. The fact that he is engaged in the currency black market, but that this is not apparent from his appearance, reflects a persistent mistrust of invisible sources of wealth: land was hard to conceal and therefore easy to tax, whereas the Crown struggled to find ways of getting revenue from mercantile riches.

Symptomatic of the pace of social change was the so-called Peasants' Revolt of 1381, actually a number of violent regional risings in Kent, East Anglia, and ultimately across the Home Counties and as far north as Yorkshire. The crisis seems to have been triggered by the introduction of a new flat-rate poll tax as the Crown desperately tried to raise more money to sustain the war with France, but the demands of the rebels were various, and by no means all the rebels were peasants. At the climax, a band of rebels marched into London, dragged the Chancellor and Treasurer of England out of the Tower of London where they were hiding, and beheaded them. They also burned down John of Gaunt's fabulous palace at the Savoy. The rebels entered London at Aldgate where Chaucer lived.

Richard II was king during the crisis of 1381. At the time he was only fourteen years old, having inherited the throne from his grandfather Edward III. Richard's father, also Edward, the Black Prince, had tragically died the year before his father. The Black Prince had been a great warrior hero and model of chivalry credited with major victories against the French in the middle of the century. Richard inherited an unstable country, impoverished by war, which he never fully controlled. His uncle, John of Gaunt, Duke of Lancaster, remained the wealthiest and most powerful man in the kingdom. After a turbulent reign Richard was finally deposed in 1399 in favour of John of Gaunt's son, who became Henry IV. Richard died in mysterious circumstances at Pontefract Castle while in the custody of, among others, Thomas Chaucer, the poet's son.

DOMESTIC LIFE

The domestic setting of *The Merchant's Tale* provides a picture of the household of a knight. It is located out of town, but within reach of it. May comes from the town, and is, therefore, socially inferior to January. A knight, though part of the landed classes, would not have had substantial an estate as a lord, and there are a number of indications throughout the tale of the scope of January's household. The marriage takes place in church, not in a private chapel such as a lord would have incorporated into his house or castle. All substantial houses were built around the hall. In earlier times the hall formed the entire house, and everyone ate, drank and slept there for safety. Gradually as activities moved out into peripheral chambers, less and less happened in the hall until it came to be the room in the house through which everyone passed on their way to somewhere else, as in traditionally constructed large houses of the nineteenth and twentieth centuries. In Chaucer's time, the function of the hall was in transition, so that here it is clear that the public business of the household was conducted in the hall, and it was where the entire household from the master of the household downwards took their meals. The master and his immediate family would eat at a table on a raised dais (see line 499) at one end of the hall, generally next to the fireplace and as far from the draughty doors to the kitchen and the outside as possible, giving rise to the expression 'high table'. Damian, the reader is particularly told, is a page or knave, meaning a young manservant, and has some privileges as he customarily carves the meat at the high table. Chaucer himself began life at court as a pageboy, working from 1356–59 in the household of the Countess of Ulster, wife to Lionel Duke of Clarence, Edward III's second son. The newly-weds go to bed in a chamber, presumably off the hall. This is a 'withdrawing room', the origin of modern 'drawing room', away from the public hall, but it is still a relatively public space. They are accompanied by well-wishers and are not truly in private until the bed curtains are closed (lines 605–610). Modern ideas of privacy and 'personal space' would have been alien to medieval people, rich and poor alike.

Private gardens in the period in which Chaucer wrote were popular but again quite unlike modern horticulture. The idea of a garden carried a number of **symbolic** resonances which have been discussed elsewhere (see Language and Style on Imagery). Dominant among these was the idea of paradise, deriving from the biblical Eden, as well as paradises in pagan mythology, and in secular romance. The major characteristic of a garden was that it was an enclosed space; a room, or rooms, in fact, but open to the air. Since the idea of the wilderness garden is strictly post-**Romantic**, it is best to think of the medieval garden in terms of very formal planting schemes threaded through with paths, with plants chosen for their aesthetic properties – either for the beauty of their flowers or their fragrance or both – their healing properties, or their **allegorical** significance. To have a garden was a mark of status, of leisure and of luxury. It was a place where the members of the household, in particular the ladies, could enjoy fresh air in safety and relative privacy, like a piece of the house moved out of doors.

LITERARY BACKGROUND

FABLIAU

The main plot, leading up to the encounter in the pear tree in *The Merchant's Tale,* derives from the **genre** of medieval narrative known as **fabliau**. The fabliau was a form of verse narrative in vogue in France in the thirteenth century, written by and for the entertainment of the nobility. It poked fun at the customs and social-climbing habits of the urban middle classes. The typical fabliau is racy in pace, often obscene in the focus of its action, and rarely if ever stops to indulge in description of character or setting. It usually centres on a practical joke, often a rude one, as the focus of the action. Its chief purpose is to make its audience laugh. If there was a pure English tradition of fabliau-telling in the same period it was oral, for little or nothing written survives.

A synopsis of the events of *The Merchant's Tale* place it in the purest tradition of fabliau. It is a protracted joke with a punchline, as an old man blinded by lust and acquisitiveness is suddenly struck physically blind, only to have his sight restored in time to see, but not to believe, that his worst fears about his young wife are realised. However in no fabliau does the narrator stop to engage in philosophical debate complete with classical, biblical and mythological references. It is unusual in fabliau to find characters by name or implication given significance beyond the particular incident in which they participate, let alone to find lengthy digressions from the main action involving supernatural beings. Chaucer's new departure is to put fabliau stories into the mouths of fabliau characters, then to lace them with versions of the embellishments more common in **romance**. Chaucer's original audience would have been courtiers, but there is evidence that as the fifteenth century progressed, his fabliau tales became popular with the upper bourgeoisie, the very class they **satirise**.

SOURCES

The Merchant's Tale, unlike many of *The Canterbury Tales*, is not a reworking of a single source, but is one of the most original of Chaucer's *Tales*. The pear tree episode occurs in a number of versions in jest-books, and particularly close parallels to Chaucer's version have been identified in German and Italian. The opening of the tale has much in common with Chaucer's *Tale of Melibee*, one of the two *Tales* told by Chaucer in his guise as a fellow pilgrim. The other material he draws on comes into the category of reference rather than source and has been noted in the Commentaries section of these Notes as it occurs. Perhaps worthy of noting again here is the *Miroir de Mariage* ('The Mirror of Marriage') by Chaucer's French contemporary, Eustace Deschamps, a long diatribe listing all the characteristics of a bad wife, and *De Raptu Proserpina* ('On the Rape of Proserpine') by Claudius Claudianus, from which he draws the story of Pluto and Proserpine.

ROMANCE

As soon as he sees May at her wedding feast, Damian becomes so overcome with love that he falls ill and has to take to his bed. He comforts himself by writing her a letter in refined verse, which he does not send but places next to his aching heart in a silk purse. When he eventually has the opportunity to declare his love to her in his enfeebled state, he swears her to secrecy. In short, Damian behaves just as the archetypal **courtly lover** should. However, the fact that he is a servant and that the object of his desires is a young woman of the town of such easy virtue that she readily succumbs to his advances and indeed takes over the plotting of the, wholly carnal, realisation of their mutual desires, leaves him up a pear tree where he belongs. As well as being a sophisticated and inventive contribution to the **fabliau** genre, *The Merchant's Tale* is a **parody** romance.

   The introduction of the heroine in aristocratic romance, the main object of desire and competition for the male protagonist, involves the convention of **effictio**. The narrative stops and she is described in physical detail using highly conventional **similes** and **metaphors**. Typically she has hair like spun gold or the rays of the sun, skin like ivory, cheeks like roses and lips like coral. If she is animated at all, she has a soft, low and tuneful voice, is moderate in all she says and does, and moves modestly. Chaucer

draws on this convention when he describes May (lines 389–98), but the
description is undercut by being set in the imagination of an old man in
bed. Heroes, too, are sometimes subject to **effictio** in romance, but always
in terms of their character and conquests rather than the finicking details
of their personal appearance. Chaucer is clearly also drawing on this
convention **satirically** when he describes the actions of Damian, who
combs and preens himself before becoming an even more unctuous servant,
when he has received May's response (lines 797–807).

Romances tend to be rather long, not only because they indulge in
long passages of static description and set piece speeches, but because of
their complicated plotting. Whereas the fabliau is a relatively simple
narrative which progresses inexorably and single-mindedly to its
punchline, the romance keeps several plots going at the same time. This
mastery of simultaneous action, which switches between location and
situation bringing them together finally for the narrative climax, was a
speciality of French romance writers and called *entrelacement* or interlacing.
Chaucer uses this technique to great comic effect, when he forces his
reader to listen to a marital dispute between the king and queen of fairies
before he finally reveals what Damian is doing up a tree.

Anti-feminism (see also under themes)

Anti-Feminism is endemic in medieval literature about relationships
between the sexes. Fundamentally, woman in the eyes of the Church
carried the blame for the loss of paradise because, according to the Book of
Genesis, Eve had accepted the fruit from the serpent in the Garden of
Eden. Eve provided the treacherous stereotype, only to be countered by the
Virgin Mary who, in being both virgin and mother, supplied an impossible
role model. In a society where many marriages were arranged, and death in
childbirth was common, many men might marry a series of women
throughout their lives, each of whom had to be of child-bearing years in
order to ensure the survival of an heir. Consequently the unsuitable
marriage of the rich but sexually feeble old man to the young, attractive
sexy woman was common in anti-feminist fiction and was known as the
senex amans, literally 'old man lover'. It in fact provides both the whole plot
and major theme of *The Merchant's Tale*. As in all such tales of *mal marié* –
literally 'badly married' – the action presupposes that the old husband is

impotent or sexually feeble. He is, therefore, jealous and keeps the young wife a virtual prisoner. She is invariably sexually frustrated. The woman is portrayed either as an unprincipled sexual opportunist or as so stupid and gullible that she can be seduced by anyone who comes along. Her husband's anxieties are then justified, for, when he is unavoidably away from home or incapacitated in some way, she flies straight into the arms of a young lover.

The anti-feminism of these accounts draws on the story of the conception of Christ in Matthew's gospel where Joseph returns from a journey, finds the Virgin Mary pregnant, but is immediately reassured of her virtue by an angel. Retellings of the Nativity, particularly in late medieval religious plays, often reflect the influence in turn of the *mal marié*, by having an unenlightened Joseph lament his lot to an audience assumed to sympathise with his plight, the common lot of all old husbands. Because most young women fall short of the Virgin Mary, elderly men should not, as January discovers, take the risk of marrying a sexy young woman. What is best for the woman is unconsidered as she is subject to the convenience of man. The close **satirical** relationship January and May have with Joseph and Mary is further emphasised by the similarity of their names. Moreover, by naming them after months, Chaucer suggests that the behaviour of these two characters is universally representative of the inevitable behaviour of those in the winter and the late spring of their lives respectively.

PART SIX

CRITICAL HISTORY AND FURTHER PERSPECTIVES

Earlier criticism of all Chaucer's fabliaux was greatly preoccupied with their obscenity; this remains an abiding preoccupation where *The Merchant's Tale* is concerned. The poet and playwright Dryden, writing in 1700, contributed more than most to the revival of interest in Chaucer, but chose to omit 'immodest' material because he saw it as his duty to instruct rather than to please. Strutt, writing about the habits of the English in 1799, condemned *The Canterbury Tales* as a pilgrimage, horrified to find them 'deficient in morality and some few outrageous to common decency'. Then, in 1818, William Hazlitt, though prepared to find humour in the licentiousness of Chaucer's comic writing and to excuse it as a product of the manners of the time, dismissed this tale simply as 'not so good as some of the others'. Criticism thereafter has, fortunately, largely ceased to confuse the values of high art with those of public morality, so that the problem of obscenity has become one of interpretation rather than censure.

Chaucer criticism has diverged into a number of distinct approaches in the second half of the twentieth century. *The Merchant's Tale* has attracted particular attention from critics who have been rereading Chaucer in relation to his historical circumstances (Marxist, New Historicist), and from a number of critics who focus on gender roles (Gender Studies). The work of many critics does not fit neatly into one category but fruitfully combines two or more approaches. The following range of approaches is not intended to be exhaustive but to represent some of the major currents of critical thought applied to *The Merchant's Tale*.

HISTORICAL CRITICISM

Critics of this type, who are numerous, use the fourteenth-century context of Chaucer's work to illuminate aspects of its meaning. At its most extreme, historical criticism searches for real life models for Chaucer's pilgrims (Manly, 1926). Most critics are less interested in that level of specificity but nonetheless focus on aspects of history to provide explanations for elements in the text. *The Merchant's Tale* is systematically studied through its links within *The Canterbury Tales*, where the main focus has been the construction of a 'marriage group' – an identifiable sub-group within the book as a whole, involving the Wife of Bath, Clerk, Merchant and Franklin – and providing the reader with a debate on the subject of marriage which is resolved by the example provided by the Franklin (Kittredge, 1912, 1915). This reading is now questioned by most critics because of its reductive effect on readings of the individual tales and because it relies heavily on an order and sequence of linking passages which manuscript studies have demonstrated is not reliably authorial. The tale is also examined through its relationship to the medieval **genres** of **fabliau** and **romance**, the sources and **analogues** for it characters and plot, and its narrative structure. The biblical allusions in the tale are explained in relation to medieval Christianity (Pittock, 1967; Robertson, 1962).

The contexts in which the genre of fabliau developed, and in which Chaucer adapted it for his own purposes, have preoccupied a number of critics (e.g. Brewer, 1975; Cooke 1978). The stratification represented particularly in *The General Prologue* has been explained in terms of contemporary satire on the medieval 'estates' system of understanding social organisation (Mann, 1973), medieval astronomy has been investigated for illumination of the tale's astrological allusions (Wood, 1970), and the heritage of medieval anti-feminism has been systematically documented (Hanna and Lawlor, 1997; Blamires, 1997).

NEW HISTORICISM

Instead of viewing historical circumstances as an illuminating context for *The Merchant's Tale*, New Historicism acknowledges the complex nature of history itself and the literary text as an historical event. Chaucer, seen by Humanist Criticism as broadminded and universal in his range of observation, is himself a phenomenon of the dynamic historical circumstances in which he lived. *The Merchant's Tale*'s apparent critique of all forms of medieval discourse and convention is class-specific: the Merchant targets the discourses of the Church and the nobility. But the teller is not in a position of total cultural alienation, as some critics suggest, for as well as mocking his authorities the Merchant also accords them respect. The Merchant typifies the class from which he comes at a particular historical moment, searching for, but unable to find, an ideology. The lack of a secure social identity in a highly stratified society leads the Merchant to display personal vulnerability. The tale enacts a search for an individual, market-based ethic which can be applied to personal relations and which is demonstrated in the debate between Pluto and Proserpine (Patterson, 1997). Conversely, the actions of Pluto and Proserpine can be seen as perpetuating an earthly conflict. Heavenly hierarchies no longer command confidence as models of human behaviour – just as earthly hierarchies in Chaucer's lifetime were increasingly being called to account for poor lordship (Strohm, 1989).

MARXIST CRITICISM

Marxist criticism also focuses on the historical dynamics in which a work of literature was written, but it concentrates particularly on evidence of tension between social classes and the economic bases of power. The economic basis for January and May's marriage is in no way abnormal. The tale demonstrates how the sacraments of the Church were being absorbed into the value systems of the marketplace. May's relationship with Damian is a search for something transcendent and is a direct product of a marriage market in which she has been sold and violated as a commodity (Aers, 1986). The love letter 'floating in the cesspit' is indicative of what people do in a world in which they treat each other as commodities. But it is not just that *The Merchant's Tale* presents social and economic truths in the plot and characters represented; Chaucer has extended the drama to the level of style, where the authentic language and imagery associated with aristocratic writing is also systematically dismantled and thrown into 'the excremental world of commodity relations'. The world governed by the imperatives of lords and of merchants is a deceptive one, and the offspring which May leads January to expect is, like contemporary social relationships, either the product of an illusion or a bastard (Knight, 1986).

HUMANIST CRITICISM

A number of critics focus on aspects of medieval literature which illuminate the human condition despite, rather than because of, historical circumstances. Chaucer uses the different **genres** available in the literature of his times to represent the manners and morals of a wide cross-section of society. The resultant achievement is artistic rather than moral. The narrative method of *The Merchant's Tale* serves to distance us from the characters. Its unity is mechanical rather than actual, but it is unrivalled as a demonstration of comic attitudes to folly (Jordan, 1967). The point of *The Merchant's Tale* is the coupling of obscenity with literary art, so that the discourse of poetry becomes the object of **satire**. The tale is an experiment in the art of disenchantment, of satire without affection for its object (David, 1976). Modern readers read too much into the relationship between the Merchant and January because of habits formed from reading novels. Once we remove the person of the narrator from his fiction we are free to read the tale as a **fabliau** full of fallible mortals, for whom sex is a healthy pleasure and in which the offenders are those who threaten the natural order and are punished by being subjected to ridicule (Stevens, 1972/73). The effects of the **imagery** of sexual possession as a form of eating, of leisurely rape and of quantities of aphrodisiac have a comic effect, but the insistence on material detail goes beyond that: to shock, as the reader glimpses a consciousness which is both disgusted and fascinated by sexuality. The tale is, thus, disturbing, and its attribution to the Merchant really solves none of the tonal problems it poses beyond an attempt to accommodate it within a conventional complaint against marriage (Pearsall in Boitani and Mann, 1986).

More extreme, so-called New Criticism sees a knowledge of the Middle Ages as largely irrelevant or unnecessary to an understanding of texts, focusing on the language itself. New Critics may openly acknowledge that they are not really describing the tale so much as their reactions to it. The 'rankness' of its rhetoric may, thus, be found 'deplorable': it juxtaposes what is potentially beautiful with ugliness and handles the contrast with perfectly realised bad taste. For example, the reductive description of the wedding ceremony is like the music of Mendelssohn played on a piano tuned flat, full of dissonances achieved by the choice of individual words. The whole is a deliberate assault on the reader's sensibilities, which makes it impossible for the attentive reader to laugh aloud because of the force of Chaucer's realisation of the Merchant's hatred (Donaldson, 1969).

GENDER STUDIES

Feminist scholarship has been very active in offering readings of Chaucer's work. *The Merchant's Tale* provides opportunities for feminist criticism as well as for a number of approaches which place issues of gender in the foreground beyond the strictly feminist. Criticism from the point of view of gender may begin simply by observing the absence of any consideration of the woman's feelings. For example, surely January is to May precisely what he rules out in his rejection of all women of thirty and above. The narrative may mock January's delusions, but it still has a consistently masculine bias, and the discussion of marriage never goes beyond considering its problems and benefits for the man. May keeps her side of the bargain by giving January her body, but nothing else. In her social position, May can only prostitute herself to January then deceive him. The models of illicit love in courtly **romance** have rendered similar arrangements respectable, but, despite the way in which the narrative parades the possibilities of its potential **analogues** drawn from literature, from the Bible and mythology, May's tragedy is that she fails to rise above a world in which relations between the sexes are a matter of bartering sex and money. The wealth of allusion does, however, also invite the reader to construct better meanings for the outcome of events than those offered by May, January or the Merchant (Martin, 1996).

The key to understanding why *The Merchant's Tale* has disturbed so many critics lies in its connection with the story of Adam and Eve told in Genesis 2, in which, unlike the account in Genesis 1, the genders are differentiated by rank, Eve being made for Adam's purposes. The tale poses the question, why, if woman was made as a mate for man, 'Lyk to himself' (line 117), does she turn out to be 'deceitful, untrustworthy and carnal'? Either humankind is innately corrupt, or woman contains something that man does not contain which requires the man to exercise control over her. The portrayal of May suggests the former because she appears to have no existence before January conjures her up from the mirror of his own imagination: woman is realised through, and is as good or as bad as, the looks and talk of men. The narrator of this tale is asserting his authority in this area over that of the other men present. Yet there is also a suggestion from the outset that there is something unknowable and uncontrollable about May. She enters the tale in a state of passivity, and the narrator admits he has no access to her feelings, then the reader is given an articulation of her judgement of January's love-making before she is finally mobilised in subversive action taken on her own initiative. The masculine counter to this threat of the uncontrolled woman is threaded through the tale in passing, but there are insistent allusions to rape, the male's fantasy of his potential to control the female through violence. By presenting the woman as both a true image of man and thus a mirror of his shortcomings, and as something potentially uncontrollable despite his superficially superior status and strength, the tale expresses the threat to the adult male identity which women present, and questions the construction of any proper gender difference (Hanson, 1992).

In radical feminist criticism, the position of the woman as something 'other' in patriarchal society, and the literary texts it generates, is extended to accompany and draw analogies from further marginalised communities and ideologies. The enclosed garden may be read as an image of the female body – closed, exclusive and difficult to secure; approachable and penetrable by a lover bold enough – but the image originates in the biblical *Song of Songs*, 4:12, a text with its own complexities because of its appropriation by Christianity from Judaism. The Jews, who were expelled from England in 1290, were a hated and marginalised group for the society in which Chaucer lived and wrote. The tale is about delusion: an old man cannot satisfy a young woman, indeed no woman can be possessed and shut away for personal enjoyment under any circumstances. Similarly the Jewish text, which carries multiple interpretations, cannot be forced into settled significations as an authority. Thus ambiguity becomes an important subtext in the tale. In *The Merchant's Tale* both femaleness and Jewishness represent communities of suppressed otherness which confront the interests of the male Christian centre (Kraman, 1997).

FURTHER READING

Information on many items in this list will be found in Critical History.

David Aers, *Chaucer, Langland and the Creative Imagination*, Routledge, 1980

— *Chaucer*, Harvester, 1986
    Marxist readings of social and economic circumstances satirised in Chaucer's work

J.J. Anderson, *Chaucer: The Canterbury Tales*, Casebook Series, Macmillan, 1974
    Selected critical commentaries, from the fifteenth to the twentieth century

Alcuin Blamires, *Women Defamed and Women Defended: An Anthology of Medieval Texts*, Oxford University Press, 1997

> Commentaries on a number of medieval anti-feminist texts, including the Wife of Bath's *Prologue*, providing sources and contexts for the Merchant and January's arguments about marriage

Piero Boitani and Jill Mann, eds, *The Cambridge Chaucer Companion*, Cambridge University Press, 1986

> Essays on a variety of aspects of Chaucer Studies including thematically organised contributions on *The Canterbury Tales*

D.S. Brewer, *Geoffrey Chaucer: Writers and their Background*, Ohio University Press, 1975

> Chaucer's writing in its historical context

John Burrow, 'Irony in *The Merchant's Tale*', *Anglia*, LXXV (1957), reproduced in Anderson, 1974 (see above)

Thomas D. Cooke, *The Old French and Chaucerian Fabliaux: A Study in their Comic Climax*, University of Missouri Press, 1978

> Historical study of Chaucer's source material

Helen Cooper, *The Canterbury Tales,* Oxford University Press, 1989

> Introduction to the tales including sources and historical context

T.W. Craik, *The Comic Tales of Chaucer*, Methuen, 1964

> Readings based on the principles of New Criticism: the tales have no meaningful references beyond themselves

Alfred David, *The Strumpet Muse: Art and Morals in Chaucer's Poetry*, Indiana University Press, 1976

E.T. Donaldson, *Speaking of Chaucer*, Athlone Press, 1970

— *Chaucer's Poetry: An Anthology for the Modern Reader,* 2nd ed. Ronald, NY, 1975

> Readings according to the principles of New Criticism

Ralph Hanna III and Traugott Lawlor, *Jankyn's Book of Wikked Wyves*, University of Georgia Press, 1997

> Two-volume reference work providing examples and commentaries on the heritage of medieval anti-feminism which supplies the sources for the Wife of Bath's *Prologue*,

which are also the sources and contexts for the Merchant and January's arguments about marriage

Elaine Tuttle Hanson, *Chaucer and the Fictions of Gender*, University of California Press, 1992

Robert Jordan, *Chaucer and the Shape of Creation: The Aesthetic Possibilities of Inorganic Structure*, Harvard University Press, 1967
> Humanist critical analysis of Chaucer's artistic achievement

George Lyman Kittredge, 'Chaucer's Discussion of Marriage', *Modern Philology*, IX (1911-12), reproduced in Anderson, 1974 (see above)

— *Chaucer and his Poetry*, Harvard University Press, 1915
> Dramatic Criticism relating tales directly to tellers

Peggy A. Knapp, *Chaucer and the Social Contest*, Routledge, 1990
> Psychoanalytical analysis based on a carnival reading of *The Merchant's Tale*

Stephen Knight, *Geoffrey Chaucer*, Basil Blackwell, 1986
> Marxist interpretation

Cynthia Kraman, 'Communities of Otherness in Chaucer's *Merchant's Tale*', in Diane Watt, ed., *Medieval Women in their Communities*, University of Wales Press, 1997

Anne Laskaya, *Chaucer's Approach to Gender in the Canterbury Tales*, D.S. Brewer, 1995

R.M. Lumiansky, *Of Sondry Folk: The Dramatic Principle in the Canterbury Tales*, University of Texas Press, 1955
> Dramatic Criticism relating tales directly to tellers

John M. Manly, *Some New Light on Chaucer*, Holt, NY, 1926
> Investigating the possibility that there were real life models for the Canterbury pilgrims

Jill Mann, *Chaucer and Medieval Estates Satire: The Literature of Social Class and the General Prologue to the Canterbury Tales*, Cambridge University Press, 1973
> Historical study arguing that the Canterbury pilgrims are satirical examples of the medieval 'estates'

Y

— *Geoffrey Chaucer: Feminist Readings,* Harvester Wheatsheaf, 1991
   Feminist reading of Chaucer

Priscilla Martin, *Chaucer's Women: Nuns, Wives and Amazons*, Macmillan, 1990

Charles Muscatine, *Chaucer and the French Tradition*, University of California Press, 1957
   Humanist reading of Chaucer's poetry against its background in medieval European literature

Lee Patterson, *Chaucer and the Subject of History,* Routledge, 1991
   New Historicist approach

Derek Pearsall, *The Life of Geoffrey Chaucer,* Blackwell, 1992
   Critical biography of Chaucer

— 'The Canterbury Tales II: Comedy', in Piero Boitani and Jill Mann, eds, *The Cambridge Chaucer Companion,* Cambridge University Press, 1986
   Humanist criticism

Malcolm Pittock, '*The Merchant's Tale*', *Essays in Criticism*, 17 (1967), 26–39.
   Historical criticism exploring the Christian contexts of the tale

D.W. Robertson, Jr., *A Preface to Chaucer: Studies in Medieval Perspectives,* Princeton University Press, 1962

Martin Stevens, 'And Venus Laugheth': An Interpretation of *The Merchant's Tale*', *Chaucer Review,* 7 (1972/73), 118-31.
   Humanist approach questioning readings which identify January too closely with the Merchant

Paul Strohm, *Social Chaucer*, Harvard University Press, 1989
   The intersection of Chaucer's writing with changing social relations in the England of his day

Chauncy Wood, *Chaucer and the Country of the Stars*, Princeton University Press, 1970
   Specialist study of Chaucer's use of astronomy

World events   Chaucer's life   Literary events

1300 Population of British Isles: *c.* 5 million

1309 Papal See moves to Avignon and comes under French control

1313 Indulgences for public sale by Pope Clement V

1315 Death of Jean de Meun, author of part 2 of *Roman de la Rose*, allegorical poem mocking love, women, the Church and those in authority

1319 Death of Jean de Joinville, French chronicler

1321 Edward II forced to abdicate, imprisoned and probably murdered. Edward III accedes to throne, with wife Philippa

1321 Death of Dante Alighieri, author of *Divine Comedy*

1330 Birth of John Gower, friend of Chaucer and author

1331 Birth of William Langland, author

1337 Birth of Jean Froissart, who will become Clerk of the Chamber to Queen Philippa, and author of *Chronicles*, a brilliant history of 14th-century Europe

1338 Beginning of 100 Years War between France and England

1341 Petrarch crowned as laureate poet at Capitol, Rome

1343? Birth of **Geoffrey Chaucer** in London

1346 French routed at Crécy by Edward III and his son the Black Prince

World events

1349 Black Death reaches England and kills one third of population

1351 First Statute of Labourers regulates wages in England

1359 Edward III makes unsuccessful bid for French throne

1361 Black Death reappears in England

1362 English becomes official language in Parliament and Law Courts

Chaucer's life

1357 Chaucer in service of Countess of Ulster, wife of Prince Lionel, 3rd son of Edward III

1359 Serves in army in France, under Prince Lionel; taken prisoner

1360 Edward III pays ransom of £16 for Chaucer's freedom

1365 Marries Philippa Pan (or Payne) de Roet

1366 In Spain on diplomatic mission

1367 Granted life pension for his services to king; birth of his son Thomas

1368 On Prince Lionel's death, his services transferred to John of Gaunt, Duke of Lancaster

Literary events

1353 In Italy, Giovanni Boccaccio finishes his *Decameron*, a collection of 100 bawdy tales

1363 Birth of Christine de Pisan, French author of *La Cité des Dames*, listing all the heroic acts and virtues of women

World events	Chaucer's life	Literary events

1369 In France with John of Gaunt's expeditionary force; begins *Book of the Duchess* on death of Blanche, John of Gaunt's wife

1370-3 Sent on diplomatic missions (11 months in Italy)

1370 *(c.)* William Langland's *Piers Plowman*

1374 Appointed Controller of the Customs and Subsidy of Wools, Skins and Leather; receives life pension from John of Gaunt

1375 *(c.) Sir Gawain and the Green Knight* written

1376 Receives payment for some secret, unspecified service

1377 Edward III dies and is succeeded by Richard II, son of the Black Prince

1377 Employed on secret missions to Flanders, and sent to France to negotiate for peace with Charles V; employed on further missions in France, Lombardy and Italy

1378 Beginning of the Great Schism: Urban VI elected Pope in Rome, Clement VII in Avignon

1380 John Wyclif, who attacked orthodox Church doctrines, condemned as heretic. Wyclif's followers translate Bible into vernacular

1380 *Parliament of Fowls* written; birth of son Lewis. Cecilia Chaumpayne releases Chaucer from charge of '*de raptu meo*'

1381 Peasants' Revolt under Wat Tyler quelled by Richard II

y

World events	Chaucer's life	Literary events
	1382 Appointed, in addition, Controller of the Petty Customs	
	1385 Allowed privilege of appointing deputy to perform his duties as Controller. Probably writes *Legend of Good Women* and *Troilus and Criseyde*	
	1385-99 Now living in Greenwich	
1386 Richard II deprived of power	**1386** Deprived of both official posts. Elected Knight of Shire of Kent	
	1387 Wife Philippa dies. Begins writing *The Canterbury Tales*	
	1388 In poverty, Chaucer sells his pensions to raise money	
1389 Richard II resumes power	**1389** Appointed clerk of king's works at Westminster	**1389** John Gower completes first version of *Confessio Amantis*
	1391 Writes *Treatise on the Astrolabe* for his son Lewis. Resigns as clerk of king's works and becomes deputy forester of royal forest at North Petherton, Somerset	
1396 John of Gaunt marries his mistress, Katherine (de Roet), Chaucer's sister-in-law		
1399 Richard II forced to abdicate. Henry IV becomes King of England		
1400 Richard II dies in prison. Population of British Isles *c.* 3.5 million	**1400** Death of Chaucer	
		1450 Gutenberg produces first printed book in moveable type

allegory a story or situation with two or more coherent meanings

ambiguity the capacity of words and sentences to have double, multiple or uncertain meanings

analogue analogy a parallel word or thing; a story with a similar or comparable plot

antithesis a rhetorical term for opposing or contrasting ideas in next-door sentences or clauses

apocrypha works of unknown authorship considered not authentic

archetype recurrent interests, situations, plots and personalities which occur in all literatures

aphorism a generally accepted principle or truth expressed in short pithy manner

apostrophe speech addressed to a person, idea or thing, often exclamatory

bathos ludicrous descent from the elevated to the ordinary and dull

burlesque the mockery of serious matter or style by dealing with a subject in a deliberately incongruous manner

circumlocution words which move round about their subject rather than announcing it directly

cliché boring phrase made tedious by constant repetition

connotation secondary meanings and overtones of a word which make metaphor possible

courtly love the conventional literary expression of ennobling and spiritual human love

denouement the final unfolding of a plot

descriptio rhetorical term for set-piece descriptive writing

dialectic logical disputation; a progress of question and answer moving towards the truth

digressio rhetorical term for narrative embellishment by a departure from the main subject which is inserted for emphasis, to attract attention and to create suspense

direct speech speech or thought reported in the first person as if in the actual words of the character

discourse a piece of writing; a framework of references relating to a specific topic or context

effictio rhetorical term for set-piece description of the hero or heroine in a narrative, usually complimentary

ellipsis the omission of words essential in the complete form of the sentence, allowing in poetry the most complete meaning in the shortest form of words

encomium a literary work written in praise of a person or noble event

euphemism concealing unpleasant, embarrassing or frightening facts or words behind words or phrases which are less blunt, rude or terrifying

fabliau comic tale in verse, characterised by bawdiness

feminine ending a line of poetry which ends with an extra lightly-stressed syllable

figure metaphor which stands for and reveals divine truths

free indirect speech a technique for narrating the thoughts or speech of a character through blending third- with first-person narrative

genre a kind or type of literature; prose, poetry, drama and their sub-divisions

grammatical gender forms or groups of nouns sharing common characteristics in certain languages, e.g. Latin, may be said to be masculine, feminine or neuter irrespective of the gender of the objects or ideas they signify

hyperbole emphasis by exaggeration

imagery language referring to objects and qualities which evoke a particular emotion or feeling

indirect speech speech or thought of a character reported in the third person with the mediation of the reporting narrator

irony saying one thing but meaning something else

lexis vocabulary

metaphor a comparison in which one thing described as being another

metonymy the substitution of the name of a thing by something closely associated with it or an attribute of it

mode a kind or manner of writing that cuts across genre; a work's approach to its subject matter

oxymoron a figure of speech in which contradictory terms are brought together in what is at first sight an impossible combination

paradox an apparently self-contradictory statement

parataxis the placing of clauses or sentences side by side without connections

parody imitation with the intent of ridicule

personification a variety of figurative language in which things or ideas are treated as if they were human beings

prolepsis anticipation of future events in narrative

protagonist the principal character or 'hero'

proverb a short popular saying embodying a general truth

pun two widely different meanings drawn out of a single word

rhetoric the art of persuasive speech or writing

rhetorical question a question asked for emphasis rather than inquiry

romance primarily medieval fictions dealing with adventures of chivalry and love

satire writing that exposes wickedness or folly by holding them up to ridicule

simile a comparison in which one thing is described as being like another

style the particular manner in which a writer expresses him- or herself, or the particular manner of a literary work

subtext implicit assumptions or situation behind the explicit plot

syntax the arrangement of words in appropriate grammatical form and order

tone the sense of a manner or mood in which a passage should be read

traductio a single word, phrase or idea enters a text in a metaphorical sense and later occurs in a literal sense

trope a word or phrase used in a sense not proper to it, thus, like metaphor, simile, or hyperbole, a departure from literal language

Pamela M. King is Professor of English, Associate Dean of Arts, Humanities and Social Sciences, and Head of the School of Culture, Media and Environment at St Martin's College, Lancaster. She is a graduate of the Universities of Edinburgh and York, and taught for several years at London University. She has published widely on aspects of medieval literature and culture, and has a particular interest in the medieval theatre.

York Notes Advanced

Margaret Atwood
Cat's Eye

Margaret Atwood
The Handmaid's Tale

Jane Austen
Emma

Jane Austen
Mansfield Park

Jane Austen
Persuasion

Jane Austen
Pride and Prejudice

Jane Austen
Sense and Sensibility

Alan Bennett
Talking Heads

William Blake
Songs of Innocence and of Experience

Charlotte Brontë
Jane Eyre

Charlotte Brontë
Villette

Emily Brontë
Wuthering Heights

Angela Carter
Nights at the Circus

Geoffrey Chaucer
The Franklin's Prologue and Tale

Geoffrey Chaucer
The Miller's Prologue and Tale

Geoffrey Chaucer
Prologue to the Canterbury Tales

Geoffrey Chaucer
The Wife of Bath's Prologue and Tale

Samuel Taylor Coleridge
Selected Poems

Joseph Conrad
Heart of Darkness

Daniel Defoe
Moll Flanders

Charles Dickens
Bleak House

Charles Dickens
Great Expectations

Charles Dickens
Hard Times

Emily Dickinson
Selected Poems

John Donne
Selected Poems

Carol Ann Duffy
Selected Poems

George Eliot
Middlemarch

George Eliot
The Mill on the Floss

T.S. Eliot
Selected Poems

T.S. Eliot
The Waste Land

F. Scott Fitzgerald
The Great Gatsby

E.M. Forster
A Passage to India

Brian Friel
Translations

Thomas Hardy
Jude the Obscure

Thomas Hardy
The Mayor of Casterbridge

Thomas Hardy
The Return of the Native

Thomas Hardy
Selected Poems

Thomas Hardy
Tess of the d'Urbervilles

Seamus Heaney
Selected Poems from Opened Ground

Nathaniel Hawthorne
The Scarlet Letter

Homer
The Iliad

Homer
The Odyssey

Aldous Huxley
Brave New World

Kazuo Ishiguro
The Remains of the Day

Ben Jonson
The Alchemist

James Joyce
Dubliners

John Keats
Selected Poems

Christopher Marlowe
Doctor Faustus

Christopher Marlowe
Edward II

Arthur Miller
Death of a Salesman

John Milton
Paradise Lost Books I & II

Toni Morrison
Beloved

George Orwell
Nineteen-Eighty-Four

Sylvia Plath
Selected Poems

Alexander Pope
Rape of the Lock and other poems

William Shakespeare
Antony and Cleopatra

William Shakespeare
As You Like It

William Shakespeare
Hamlet

William Shakespeare
King Lear

William Shakespeare
Macbeth

William Shakespeare
Measure for Measure

William Shakespeare
The Merchant of Venice

William Shakespeare
A Midsummer Night's Dream

William Shakespeare
Much Ado About Nothing

William Shakespeare
Othello

William Shakespeare
Richard II

William Shakespeare
Richard III

William Shakespeare
Romeo and Juliet

William Shakespeare
The Taming of the Shrew

William Shakespeare
The Tempest

William Shakespeare
Twelfth Night

William Shakespeare
The Winter's Tale

George Bernard Shaw
Saint Joan

Mary Shelley
Frankenstein

Jonathan Swift
Gulliver's Travels and A Modest Proposal

Alfred, Lord Tennyson
Selected Poems

Virgil
The Aeneid

Alice Walker
The Color Purple

Oscar Wilde
The Importance of Being Earnest

Tennessee Williams
A Streetcar Named Desire

Jeanette Winterson
Oranges Are Not the Only Fruit

John Webster
The Duchess of Malfi

Virginia Woolf
To the Lighthouse

W.B. Yeats
Selected Poems

Metaphysical Poets

GCSE and equivalent levels

Maya Angelou
I Know Why the Caged Bird Sings

Jane Austen
Pride and Prejudice

Alan Ayckbourn
Absent Friends

Elizabeth Barrett Browning
Select Poems

Robert Bolt
A Man for All Seasons

Harold Brighouse
Hobson's Choice

Charlotte Brontë
Jane Eyre

Emily Brontë
Wuthering Heights

Shelagh Delaney
A Taste of Honey

Charles Dickens
David Copperfield

Charles Dickens
Great Expectations

Charles Dickens
Hard Times

Charles Dickens
Oliver Twist

Roddy Doyle
Paddy Clarke Ha Ha Ha

George Eliot
Silas Marner

George Eliot
The Mill on the Floss

Anne Frank
The Diary of Anne Frank

William Golding
Lord of the Flies

Oliver Goldsmith
She Stoops to Conquer

Willis Hall
The Long and the Short and the Tall

Thomas Hardy
Far from the Madding Crowd

Thomas Hardy
The Mayor of Casterbridge

Thomas Hardy
Tess of the d'Urbervilles

Thomas Hardy
The Withered Arm and other Wessex Tales

L.P. Hartley
The Go-Between

Seamus Heaney
Selected Poems

Susan Hill
I'm the King of the Castle

Barry Hines
A Kestrel for a Knave

Louise Lawrence
Children of the Dust

Harper Lee
To Kill a Mockingbird

Laurie Lee
Cider with Rosie

Arthur Miller
The Crucible

Arthur Miller
A View from the Bridge

Robert O'Brien
Z for Zachariah

Frank O'Connor
My Oedipus Complex and Other Stories

George Orwell
Animal Farm

J.B. Priestley
An Inspector Calls

J.B. Priestley
When We Are Married

Willy Russell
Educating Rita

Willy Russell
Our Day Out

J.D. Salinger
The Catcher in the Rye

William Shakespeare
Henry IV Part 1

William Shakespeare
Henry V

William Shakespeare
Julius Caesar

William Shakespeare
Macbeth

William Shakespeare
The Merchant of Venice

William Shakespeare
A Midsummer Night's Dream

William Shakespeare
Much Ado About Nothing

William Shakespeare
Romeo and Juliet

William Shakespeare
The Tempest

William Shakespeare
Twelfth Night

George Bernard Shaw
Pygmalion

Mary Shelley
Frankenstein

R.C. Sherriff
Journey's End

Rukshana Smith
Salt on the Snow

John Steinbeck
Of Mice and Men

Robert Louis Stevenson
Dr Jekyll and Mr Hyde

Jonathan Swift
Gulliver's Travels

Robert Swindells
Daz 4 Zoe

Mildred D. Taylor
Roll of Thunder, Hear My Cry

Mark Twain
Huckleberry Finn

James Watson
Talking in Whispers

Edith Wharton
Ethan Frome

William Wordsworth
Selected Poems

A Choice of Poets

Mystery Stories of the Nineteenth Century including The Signalman

Nineteenth Century Short Stories

Poetry of the First World War

Six Women Poets